EID MUBARAK!
ISLAMIC
CELEBRATION AROUND
THE WORLD

A Supplementary Social Studies Unit for Grade One

Written by Susan Douglass
Illustrated by Abd al-Muttalib Fahema

Goodword**kidz**
Helping you build a family of faith

First published 1995 by
The International Institute of Islamic Thought (IIIT)
500 Grove St., 2nd Floor
Herndon, VA 20170-4735, USA
Tel: (1-703) 471 1133 / Fax: (1-703) 471 3922
E-mail: iiit@iiit.org / URL: http://www.iiit.org

First published by Goodword Books in 2003
Reprinted 2004
in arrangement with The International Institute of Islamic Thought
© The International Institute of Islamic Thought 1995

Goodword Books Pvt. Ltd.
1, Nizamuddin West Market
New Delhi 110 013
e-mail: info@goodwordbooks.com
Printed in India

www.goodwordbooks.com

INTERNATIONAL INSTITUTE OF ISLAMIC THOUGHT (IIIT)

Islamic School Book Project

IIIT is a cultural and intellectual foundation registered in the United States of America in 1981 with the objectives of providing a comprehensive Islamic outlook through elucidating the principle of Islam and relating them to relevant issues of contemporary thought; regaining the intellectual, cultural, and civilizational identity of the ummah through Islamization of the various disciplines of knowledge, to rectify the methodology of contemporary Islamic thought in order to enable it to resume its contribution to the progress of human civilization and give it meaning and direction in line with the values and objectives of Islam.

IIIT seeks to achieve its objectives by holding specialized academic seminars and conferences, supporting educational and cultural institutions and projects, supporting and guiding graduate and post-graduate studies.

The IIIT Islamic School Book Project supports the writing, publication, and distribution of books and other teaching material for schools as part of its effort to present the true picture of Islam in a factual objective way. These educational resources, developed under the general guidelines of the IIIT Islamization of Knowledge program, cover the following fields: Islamic Studies, Social Studies, Literature, Science and Mathematics. International collaboration and coordination with teachers, schools and organizations is assured through the International Forum for Education Resources for Islamic English-medium schools.

For more information contact:

The Director
IIIT Islamic School Book Project
International Institute of Islamic Thought (IIIT)
500 Grove St., 2nd Floor,
Herndon, VA 20170-4735, USA
Tel: (1-703) 471 1133 / Fax: (1-703) 471 3922
E-mail: iiit@iiit.org / URL: http://www.iiit.org

Susan Douglass is an American-born Muslim who accepted Islam in 1974. She received the Bachelor of Arts in History from the University of Rochester in 1972. She received the Master of Arts in Arab Studies from Georgetown University in 1992. She holds teaching certification in social studies from New York and Virginia.

She has taught in a variety of settings and subjects, beginning with volunteer work in Headstart in 1965. She taught and coordinated art classes in a summer youth program from 1970-72 in Rochester, NY. Since returning to the U.S. in 1984, from extended stays in Germany and Egypt, she resumed work in education. She has taught arts, crafts and story sessions in Muslim summer school programs for several years in Herndon, VA. As teacher and Head of the Social Studies Department at the Islamic Saudi Academy, Fairfax, VA, she taught both elementary and secondary social studies, built a supplementary resource library, and led in preparing a K-12 social studies curriculum utilizing both American and Arab resources for the Academy's accreditation. The current IIIT project was conceived and developed in the classroom. The author is involved in numerous other educational projects, including work as reviewer and consultant to major textbook publishers in the field of social studies. She has reviewed and offered revisions to the California History/Social Science Framework (1994) and the National History Standards Project (1994), in addition to various projects for the Council on Islamic Education in Fountain Valley, CA, including a book, *Strategies and Structures for Presenting World History, with Islam and Muslim History as a Case Study* (Council on Islamic Education, 1994.)

ADVISORY PANEL MEMBERS

Rahima Abdullah
Elementary Coordinator
Islamic Saudi Academy, Alexandria, VA

Dr. Kadija A. Ali
Educational Projects Coordinator
International Institute of Islamic Thought,
Herndon, VA

Jinan N. Alkhateeb
Social Studies Teacher
Islamic Saudi Academy, Alexandria, VA

Mrs. Hamida Amanat
Director of Education
American Islamic Academy
Curriculum Consultant
Al-Ghazaly School, Pine brook, NJ

Shaker El Sayed
Coordinator
Islamic Teaching Center, Islamic Schools
Department
Islamic Society of North America,
Plainfield, IN

Dr. Tasneema Ghazi
IQRA International Educational Foundation,
Chicago, IL

Dr. Zakiyyah Muhammad
Universal Institute of Islamic Education,
Sacramento, CA

ACKNOWLEDGEMENTS

Many people's efforts have contributed to producing this series of supplementary units for Social Studies. First, I am grateful to the International Institute of Islamic Thought (IIIT) for placing their confidence in me to undertake a project of this size and for providing all the financial and logistical resources needed for its completion. I would like to thank Dr. Mahmud Rashdan, under whose guidance this project began in 1988. His wisdom helped to set it on a solid foundation. Without constant support and encouragement by Dr. Omar Kasule, project director 1991-present, and Dr. Khadija Ali Sharief, project coordinator (1993-present), this unit would never have met the light of day.

The project has been much enhanced by the members of the Advisory Panel. In addition to offering guidance on the project as a whole, they have spent much time and detailed effort on each individual manuscript. These brothers and sisters are all active education professionals with a broad range of experience and a long list of accomplishments.

May Allah reward my family and grant them patience for sacrificing some degree of comfort so that I, as wife and mother, might realize this goal. I owe special thanks to my husband, Usama Amer, for his constant help with the computer, with Arabic sources and many other matters of consultation. With regard to the research, writing and editing process, I especially thank the brothers and sisters from the countries discussed in the unit, who provided research materials, sketches, personal photographs and first-hand recollections of the customs related here. They are Usama Amer, my husband (Egypt), Qadar Chang (China), Shahran Gasem (Malaysia), Aminata Sallah and Aisha Gaye (Gambia), Marziyeh Bastani (Iran), Tanweer Mirza (Pakistan), Sabiha al-Barzinji (Turkey), M.K. Hussein and Saadia Muhammad (Trinidad). Many others provided information, including most of those whose names are listed on this page. I also thank the teachers who read the manuscript at early stages. They are Mary Al-Khatib and Jalees Rahim. Gratitude is extended to Rabiah Abdullah, whose keen mind and sharp pencil have shaped and pruned text for the whole project as well as lending her encouragement since its inception. Thanks also to the numerous children who read this unit in manuscript form, and to Rahima Abdullah, an advisory panel member who used it in one of her classes.

It has been a pleasure to work on several units with the illustrator, Abd al-Muttalib Fahema, who worked with skill and dedication, bringing enthusiasm and a rare willingness to go the extra mile to research a sketch or detail for accuracy. Finally, thanks to the many people of Kendall/Hunt Publishing Co. who graciously met my many requests and turned tentative, complex and unfamiliar material into a finished product.

May Allah reward the efforts of sincere workers and of the teachers and students for whom this unit was written.

Susan Douglass
Falls Church, Virginia
January 1995

TABLE OF CONTENTS

Part I:

Teacher's Notes

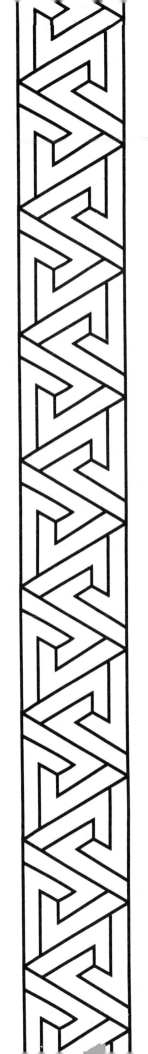

INTRODUCTION

This unit is the second in a series of supplementary units for use in Muslim school K-12 Social Studies programs. The underlying assumption is that most such schools will use mainstream curricula as a starting point. While it is certainly desirable and necessary to produce a complete Islamic Social Studies curriculum, it is a task best taken on step-by-step. In the meantime, it seems most productive to design supplements which are integrated into topics typically studied at a given grade level, while introducing content vital to the development of Muslim identity, values and world view. At the same time, it is hoped that the issues covered in these units are of such importance that they might become integrated into a complete Islamic curriculum.

An important requirement in the design of this supplementary series is that each unit feature skills and concepts typical for the scope and sequence of the social studies curriculum in its grade level. In this way, the teacher can introduce information about the Islamic heritage using material that is well integrated into the existing social studies program. This feature of the design also makes it possible to substitute this material for unsatisfactory or unnecessary material from standard textbooks, thus avoiding overburdening the students.

PURPOSE AND PLACEMENT OF THE UNIT

This supplementary unit describes the two Islamic celebrations, their background and major features of their observance. It shows what, when, why and how Muslims celebrate on these two occasions, and gives a sense of their inherent values. The unit is also a case study of the unity and diversity of Muslims across the globe, an enjoyable introduction to some customs in selected countries where Muslims live and their geography.

Countries were selected to include both majority and minority Muslim populations, to present a range of countries across the globe, and to represent a variety of the many ethnic groups and geographic features that make up the Muslim world community. No attempt has been made to comprehensively cover all countries, cultures or customs, as this is far beyond the scope of a unit for the primary grades. By selecting certain countries, others were necessarily excluded, although they might have served equally well. To rectify this unfortunate shortcoming, activities have been suggested that can enhance coverage to include all the nationalities represented in an individual teacher's classroom. At the same time, such a project increases student participation. All of the customs related here have either been witnessed by the author in various countries, or they were related personally by Muslims from those countries, who also assisted with the illustrations and diagrams for each custom. Finally, no attempt has been made to cover all of the customs of the country selected; rather, they were selected for variety, attractiveness to the target age group and for their relevance to and illustration of certain social studies concepts which are brought out in the teaching suggestions.

In terms of the overall objectives of a social studies curriculum for first grade, the teacher will find that many skills and concepts from the first grade year are introduced or reviewed in this unit. It is recommended that the unit be placed near or between the two holidays if these fall during the school year calendar. Alternatively, the unit can serve as an addition to or substitute for standard textbook units on holidays around the world, and offers an interesting contrast and complement to such units. In reading and skill level, it corresponds roughly to the second half of the first grade year, where such holiday units are often placed.

The student text and corresponding teaching suggestions are arranged into five sections:

Introduction: Sets the scene with universality of celebration, various occasions, and Muslim religion.

Section 1 introduces the Arabic word "eid" (a simpler transliteration selected in favor of the more common 'id), defines its celebration as universal to Muslims, describes its origin in Qur'an and Sunnah and names the two Islamic celebrations.

Section 2 tells when 'id celebrations occur. A simple description of the lunar calendar is given.

Section 3 names each 'id, describes the occasion for its observance, its background, meaning and some of its inherent values.

Section 4 describes universal practices of Muslims in preparation for and observance of 'id.

Section 5 describes unique 'id customs in 10 different countries across the globe. Each is used to bring out a point about Islamic values, the geography of Muslim countries or a specific social studies concept.

The student will:

Introduction:
- appreciate the universality of celebration among people everywhere.
- list some common occasions for celebration.
- list some common features of celebration.
- identify Muslims religion, their book and prophet.

Section 1:
- tell how often Muslims celebrate.
- define "eid" as the Arabic word for a day of celebration.
- define 'id as an Islamic celebration observed by all Muslims.
- name the sources for Muslims' knowledge of what and when to celebrate.

Section 2:
- tell when Muslims celebrate 'id.
- understand that 'id occurs in different seasons.
- understand that the moon and sun are used to tell time.

Section 3:
- name the two annual 'id celebrations.
- name the occasion for each 'id.
- describe the background of each 'id.
- understand some aspects of the meaning and values behind each 'id.
- describe how and why Muslims fast in Ramadan.
- describe the Hajj in simple terms.
- name the persons commemorated in the Hajj story.

Section 4:
- tell how Muslims everywhere prepare for 'id celebrations.
- describe 'id prayer services.
- describe universal elements of Islamic celebrations.
- explain the importance of Islamic celebrations.

Section 5:
- name the countries and locate them on the outline map by shape and size.
- identify the continent on which each country is located.
- identify the geographic and cultural features of the countries described.
- describe customs in the countries named.
- describe some customs unique to the students' own families or countries.
- explain some meanings of Muslim 'id customs.

The activities described here are intended for use with the Eid Mubarak! student text. The text segment of this binder is designed to be reproduced for each student. The illustrations in the booklet may be colored in by the children and taken home to keep as a reminder of their study. The teacher may direct an activity to make simple or elaborate bindings for the booklet.

The teaching suggestions provide comprehension exercises, development and reinforcement of skills and concepts introduced in the text, and enrichment activities for social studies with springboards to other disciplines. They are designed to offer maximum flexibility in expanding or compressing the unit to fit variable time frames. The suggestions are organized according to sections of the text, and are labeled by type of activity:

PRE-READING: These activities are done before classroom reading in the student text. Their purpose is to provide background information, define unfamiliar vocabulary words and terms, and establish a receptive frame of mind in the students.

COMPREHENSION: These activities are completed after each section is read. They include questions for classroom discussion and group or individual work, explanatory background material to be provided by the teacher, and exercises related to understanding the content.

LEARNING NEW CONCEPTS: The focus is on comprehension and manipulation of a concept from the social studies disciplines. The concept is explained, put to use and reinforced in these activities.

ACQUIRING SKILLS: These activities feature social studies skills such as interpreting information from maps, diagrams and pictures; reading, writing, thinking and study skills, and citizenship.

ENRICHMENT: Activities are offered which build upon the basic lessons, adding depth and enjoyment to the learning experience. They may include art, science or math projects, literature for additional reading, dramatic or role play.

This supplementary unit is designed for flexibility of implementation. The bare-bones unit, covering only the student text, pre-reading and comprehension activities, is designed for implementation within a two- to three-week time frame. Alternatively, the teacher may choose to cover all of Sections 1, 2 and 3, for example, but only a few of the customs from Section 4, selecting some of the concept, skills and enrichment activities. Most teachers will select some areas for light coverage, using more activities for depth in other sections of the unit. The teacher may choose to utilize the unit for broader purposes over a longer time period. A wide variety of objectives from the social studies curriculum for the first grade year are touched upon or even covered in the concept and skills activities. Crossover projects to language arts, math and science have also been liberally included.

Part II:

Student Text

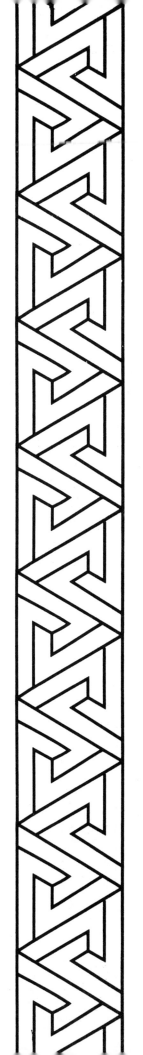

"EID MUBARAK!" HOW MUSLIMS CELEBRATE AROUND THE WORLD

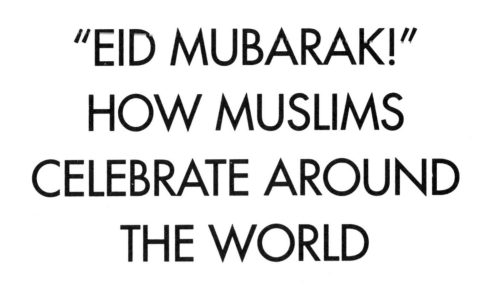

Written by Susan Douglass
illustrated by Abd al-Muttalib Fahema

لِكُلِّ أُمَّةٍ جَعَلْنَا مَنسَكًا هُمْ نَاسِكُوهُ

To each nation we have given sacred rites to perform... (Qur'an 22:67)

What Is This Book About?

People everywhere have special days.
People celebrate many different things.
They celebrate seasons of the year.
They celebrate births and weddings.
They celebrate important events and people.
They celebrate belief in God.

On special days, people join together to celebrate.
They stop working and have fun together.
They visit and share special foods.
They wear their best clothes.

Muslims have special days, too.
Families celebrate births, weddings and other things.
All Muslims celebrate twice each year.
They enjoy Islamic celebrations.
Islam is the name of Muslims' religion.
The *Qur'an* is their holy book.
Prophet Muhammad ﷺ is their teacher.

You will learn in this book how Muslims celebrate.

What Do Muslims Celebrate?

Muslims celebrate twice each year.
A day of celebration in Arabic is *eid*.
Muslims everywhere celebrate *eid*.
The *Qur'an* and Prophet Muhammad ﷺ teach Muslims about *eid*.

The first *eid* is called *Eid al-Fitr*.
The second *eid* is called *Eid al-Adha*.

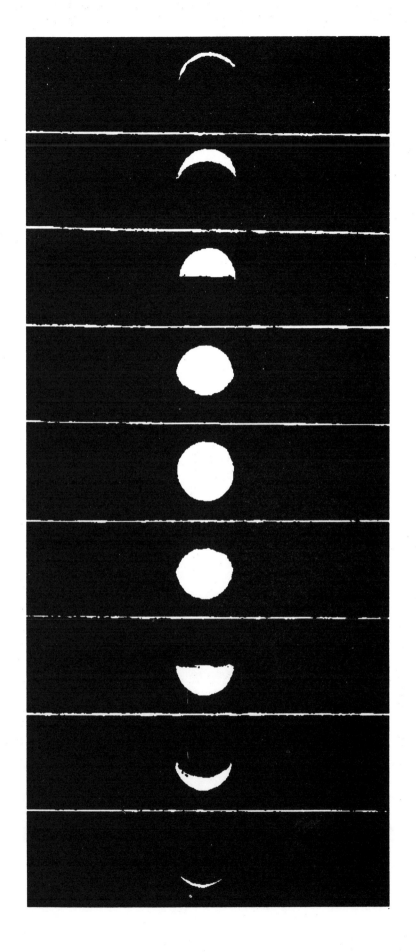

When is *Eid* Celebrated?

Islamic *eid* comes each year.
It comes in different seasons.
Sometimes *eid* comes in summer.
It comes in spring, autumn or winter.

The Islamic calendar changes with the moon.
The moon's shape changes each month.
Look how the moon changes!

What is the story of *Eid?*

Eid al-Fitr

The first celebration is **Eid al-Fitr**.
It starts on the first day of the month called *Shawwal*.
Eid al-Fitr comes after the month called *Ramadan*.

During *Ramadan*, Muslims **fast**.
They do not eat anything.
They do not drink anything.
They **fast** from dawn to sundown.
After sundown they share break-fast.
Then everyone prays.

The *Qur'an* and the Prophet teach Muslims to fast.
Fasting helps Muslims think about poor people.
Fasting helps Muslims learn to be strong.
Fasting is good for our bodies.
Fasting helps Muslims remember Allah at all times.

All Muslims **fast** together for one month.
Then they celebrate *Eid al-Fitr*.

Eid al-Adha

The second celebration is **Eid al-Adha**.
Muslims sacrifice animals on **Eid al-Adha**.
They say "bismillah" and "Allahu Akbar."
They keep some meat.
They give some to friends and family.
They give some to poor people.

Eid al-Adha comes at the end of the **Hajj**.
Hajj is a trip to Makka.
Muslims want to make **Hajj**.
Hajj is a trip to Makka.
Muslims want to make *hajj* once in their lives.
They visit the **Kaaba** in Makka.
Prophet Ibrahim built the **Kaaba**.
Muslims visit places where Ibrahim and his family went.

Eid al-Adha celebrates stories of Ibrahim.
Muslims remember how Ibrahim obeyed Allah.
They remember how Allah helped Ibrahim's family.
They remember Ibrahim, his son and his wife Hajar.
Do you know the story of Ibrahim's family?

How Do All Muslims Celebrate *Eid?*

Getting Ready

Before *Eid*, everyone cleans their homes.
They make sweets.
They cook special food.
The special food is for *Eid*.

Everyone takes a bath.
They wear nice, colorful clothes.
Many children get new shoes.

Eid Prayer

Families go to the *Eid* prayer.
The prayer is outdoors or in the *masjid*.
All the Muslims pray to *Allah*.
They listen quietly to the imam's talk.

After prayer, Muslims greet each other.
Children get gifts, candy and money.
Friends, family and neighbors visit.
They eat good food together.
They give food and money to poor people.

What Are Some *Eid* Customs Around the World?

You have read how all Muslims celebrate *Eid*.
Now, you will read about special ways to celebrate.
Muslims in each country have different customs.
They have fun in different ways.
There are many more countries and customs.
These are only a few.
Muslims live all over the world.

Pakistan

Pakistan is a Muslim country in Asia.
It has very high mountains.

The stars sparkle at night.
The sky is clear in the mountains.
It is the end of *Ramadan*.
Families watch for the new moon.
They watch on top of their houses.
Street singers go through the streets.
People hug each other.
The children like to stay up late.
They help to get ready for *Eid*.

On the day of *Eid*, people wear fancy clothes.
Women and girls paint henna on hands and feet.
Children get money and gifts.
They enjoy swings and rides.

Iran

Iran is a Muslim country in Asia.
Its *masjid* are beautiful.

It is the night before *Eid*.
The children have shiny, new shoes.
The children are very excited.
They put the shoes under their pillow.
They dream about *Eid* tomorrow.

Egypt

Egypt is a Muslim country in Africa.
The world's longest river is in Egypt.
Many people live in Egypt.

In *Ramadan*, children get colored lanterns.
The children have a parade.
They hold the lanterns high.
They sing songs.
Neighbors give them gifts.

On *Eid*, colored lights decorate houses and shops.
Children wear clothes in bright colors.
Families go to parks.
They play and eat together.
They ride horses and swings, laugh and have fun.
Everyone enjoys *Eid*.

Turkey

Turkey is a Muslim country between Europe and Asia.
Turkey has mountains and coasts.
It has farms and big cities.

In *Ramadan*, Muslims eat a meal before dawn.
It is still dark outside.
A drummer walks through the streets.
Sleeping people hear his drum.
Boom-ba-ba-boom! Boom-ba-ba-boom!
Wake up to eat!
Wake up to pray!

On *Eid*, the drummer comes again.
People give him sweets and money.

Holland

Holland is a small country in Europe.
Few Muslims live there.

Muslims in Holland have an Islamic school.
The children in the class make a *Ramadan* box.
Everyone puts in a gift.
On *Eid*, they open the box.
Everyone gets a different gift.
They greet and thank each other.

United States

The United States is in North America.
It is a large country.
Muslims from many countries live there.

On *Eid*, Muslims meet in parks or *masjid*.
They pray the *Eid* prayer.
After prayer, children get balloons.
They ride ponies.
They have fun on carnival rides.
Families have picnics.

Trinidad

Trinidad is near South America.
Trinidad is a beautiful island.

Muslims came to Trinidad long ago.
Their grandfathers came from Africa.
Their grandfathers came from India.
Many Muslims live in Trinidad.
Christians and Hindus live there, too.

On *Eid*, everyone has the day off.
Schools close. Offices close.
Muslim families celebrate *Eid*.
They go to prayer.
They buy sweets.
They visit each other's homes.
Christians and Hindus come to visit, too.
Muslims send sweets to neighbors.
Television shows Islamic programs all day.

Malaysia

Malaysia is a Muslim country in Asia.
Part of Malaysia is on a peninsula.
A peninsula has water on three sides.
Part of Malaysia is on an island.

Malaysia is a warm, rainy country.
Rice, bamboo and coconuts grow there.

It is the day before *Eid*.
Families cook special rice
They cook it inside hollow bamboo stalks.
They mix the rice with coconut milk.
They hang the bamboo over a big fire.
The rice cooks all day.
The children play and laugh.
They like the big fire.

China

China is in Asia.
China is a very large country.
Many Muslims live in China.

Muslims share special bread on *Eid*.
They make dough from flour.
They fry the dough in hot oil.

Chinese Muslims know a story about the bread.
A poor woman made bread for Prophet Muhammad ﷺ .
She had only a little flour.
She had only a little oil.
The Prophet tasted the woman's bread.
It tasted very good.
It was good because she loved the Prophet.
Prophet Muhammad ﷺ thanked and blessed her.

Gambia

Gambia is a Muslim country in Africa.
It is near the ocean.

Families live together in groups.
They share water from a well.
They plant fruit trees.

For *Eid al-Adha*, the families buy sheep.
The children are very happy.
They bring grass and water for the sheep.
Children help their fathers sacrifice the sheep.
They cut the meat.
They give some meat to other families.
Each child takes some to neighbors.

In each house, families cook pots of food.
Women carry the pots on their heads.
They put the pots under a big tree.
Everyone wears new clothes.
Everyone brings a chair and a spoon.
The whole family shares the food.

Part III:

Teaching Suggestions & Enrichment Activities

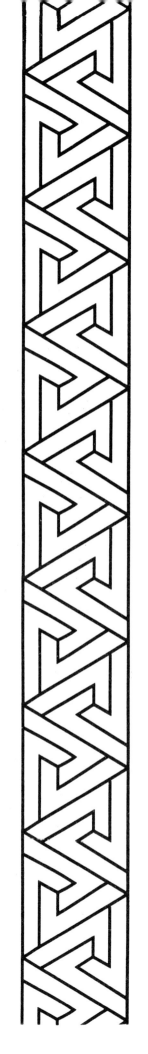

INTRODUCTION: WHAT IS THIS BOOK ABOUT?

UNIT PRE-READING:

1. Discuss various words for occasions such as holiday, festival, celebration, feast.

2. Discuss what people do on special days. Explain that the class will study when Muslims have these special days, and what they do to celebrate.

SECTION 1: WHEN DO MUSLIMS CELEBRATE EID?

COMPREHENSION:

1. Explain that in Arabic, the language of the Qur'an, a day of celebration is "eid". Please note that this transliteration, while imperfect, was preferred over the more standard 'id because it contains no non-letter characters that might confuse new readers. It is assumed that the teacher will help with correct pronunciation. Use Worksheet #1 to trace and color the word in Arabic script.

2. Reinforce and explain how Muslims know about 'id, from the combined information in the Qur'an and the example and explanation of Prophet Muhammad ﷺ.

LEARNING NEW CONCEPTS:

1. Celebration is the central concept in the Introduction and Section 1. By eliciting the students' experiences, develop a definition of the term in three stages, to include:

   - kinds of celebration (weddings, births, deaths, special events, anniversaries, etc.)

   - why people celebrate (to have a break from everyday life and work, to be happy and have fun, to remember important things together, to share friendship and things they have like food and gifts)

   - what people do to celebrate (being together, visiting, sharing special foods and gifts, etc.)

2. Emphasize that the source of Islamic holidays is the Qur'an, and the practice of Prophet Muhammad, who first celebrated 'id in the community. Discuss one purpose of celebrations, that Allah gave people a break from everyday life and work. During the break, people remember important things together. They share and think about others. People can be happy, be together, have fun.

3. Elaborate upon kinds of celebration, their meaning and significance. Explain that celebration means sharing happiness together, thanking Allah for His gifts and reminding each other of important things. Explain that the two 'ids are the only

times when all Muslims celebrate together. Other examples of smaller, individual celebrations are:

- Weddings

- Birth of new babies, birthday anniversaries (Celebration of birthdays is not accepted practice in Islam, as Muhammad did not celebrate this occasion)

- Funerals (to help people who lose loved ones, say good-bye to people who have died and to pray for them)

- Anniversaries of important events

4. Ask the students to draw pictures of celebration to stimulate discussion of what happens in a celebration. Have each child explain his/her drawing, then make a list, which might include the following

- Sharing with people we know and people we don't know

- Having fun

- Feeling "like new"

- Remembering Allah's prophets, belief in Allah, obedience to Allah

- Remembering important things which have happened

In the course of the unit, the teacher will explain that Muslims celebrate important values, not people.

NOTE: Muslims don't have many holidays, only two each year, each of which lasts several days. Muslims celebrate sometimes, but should live simply, work hard all year, and not waste time and money.

SECTION 2: WHEN DO MUSLIMS CELEBRATE EID?

PRE-READING/COMPREHENSION:

1. Explain that students will learn how Muslims know when 'id comes on the Islamic calendar.

2. Review and build upon previous knowledge of the calendar and the seasons. Students should name the months of each season and identify their dates of birth and major local or national holidays on a calendar.

3. Pointing to a typical solar calendar, explain in simplest terms that it changes with movement of the earth and sun during the year. Explain that Muslims use a different calendar in which the months are not always in the same season. The Islamic calendar changes with the moon.

ACQUIRING SKILLS: Different calendars that change with the moon or the sun

4. Introduce the lesson by asking students why we need to know the date, days of the week and months of the year. The class should agree that they need to know when to do things, especially things that people do together, like going to school in September, having summer vacation in June, planting gardens in the spring, etc.

5. Explain that Muslims must study the world around them to learn to tell time, so everyone can know when to do things. Ask: What kinds of things do Muslims need to know time for? (Daily prayers, Friday prayers, and 'id celebration). Explain that the Qur'an tells Muslims about using the sun and moon to tell time. Now and long ago, people watched and noticed changes in position of sun and moon, shape of the moon. They noticed a pattern that repeats. They used these patterns to make calendars — one using the sun's pattern, and one using the moon's pattern. (See lesson plan below, "Enrichment," for demonstration of science behind the calendar.) Muslims use both kinds, but the Islamic holidays are set by the moon calendar. Use Worksheet # 6 to learn the 12 months of the Islamic calendar year.

ENRICHMENT: Science lesson on the motion of the sun and moon

6. Make a simple model of the earth using a flashlight on a globe in a darkened room. Show how the sun shines on different parts of the earth during different seasons. You need not explain rotation and revolution; just explain part of the phenomenon. Tell the students as much as you feel they can absorb about the relationship between the strength of the sun's rays on earth and the seasons, as well as the length of the year.

7. Using a styrofoam sphere or other ball, show how the moon goes around the earth. Show how the sun's light causes the earth's shadow on the moon, using a simple Styrofoam, clay or playball model. Demonstrate that it takes about 29-30 days, one month, for the moon to travel around the earth. Explain that the shape of this shadow on the moon helps us count months. Using the illustration on page #14, show the pattern from new moon to full moon to new moon. Make a sliding model of the phases of the moon, using Worksheet #5 and a business envelope cut as shown.

8. You may wish to explore with the students the way the moon calendar changes with respect to the sun calendar, so that the Islamic celebrations happen in different seasons of the year over time. Using a calendar, identify some holidays familiar to the students by month, day and season in which they fall. Have students ask parents when Ramadan and 'Id al-Adha came last year. Find out when they will come this year. Compare dates. The children will be familiar with the varying lengths of a month from 28 days (February) to 31 days (January, May, etc.). Explain that moon months are shorter. That way, 12 moon months are shorter than 12 months on the sun calendar. So the 'id days seem to move backward through the seasons, coming a little earlier each year. Explain that since Muslims live all over the world, this

is the fairest way Allah could make the celebration days, a mercy from Allah. Muslims fast sometimes in summer and sometimes in winter. It is fair for people all over the world, since they take turns fasting during long, hot summer days and short, cool winter days.

SECTION 3: WHAT IS THE STORY OF THE TWO EIDS?

PRE-READING:

1. Have students list celebrations they know about from any culture, such as Columbus Day, birthdays, etc. (without being concerned at the moment about the content). Explain that every special occasion has a meaning and a story. Give examples of the meaning of some of the holidays mentioned, such as the birth or death of a famous person (Note here that many Muslims have a custom of celebrating Prophet Muhammad's birthday [Mawlid an-Nabi], but scholars agree that this has no basis in the Prophet's own example.) Muslims also commemorate two journeys, al-Isra wal-Miraj, the Prophet's night journey to Jerusalem, and the hijra, or migration of the Prophet and his companions from Makkah to Madinah.

COMPREHENSION :

2. Practice saying the name of each 'id. Use Worksheet #2 to say and trace the names of the two eids.

3. Identify Ramadan as the name of a month in the Islamic lunar calendar. You may write the word in Arabic on the chalkboard.

LEARNING NEW CONCEPTS:

4. Fasting — Use the text definition as a basis for discussion. Elicit the students' experiences with fasting, their own or others'. Ask whether the students think fasting is difficult or easy. The following discussion will answer the three questions — how, when and why Muslims fast.

   - HOW: Ask the students what Muslims do not do when fasting? (eat or drink) Students may also take the opportunity to say that a fasting person does not argue, use bad language or do bad things. What do they do? (pray extra prayers, think about Allah, do good deeds, share with others) Ask whether fasting is done alone or with others.

   - WHEN: Use clues from text to evaluate comprehension. Ask: Do Muslims fast for a long time? During the day? At night? How many days? Remind students of the Islamic calendar, Ramadan being a month. Explain iftar and the 'id Al-Fitr feast at the end of the month. The origin of the familiar word break-fast might be explained.

- WHY: Encouraging students to use textual clues, discuss the source of Islamic fasting in Qur'an and Sunnah. State that fasting during Ramadan is one of the most important duties for a Muslim, a pillar of Islam. Discuss who must fast, i.e. a healthy, grown-up person who is not travelling. Using discretion, the teacher might chose to mention that women who are expecting or nursing a baby may, but need not fast in Ramadan. The situation may be found in the students' own families. Teach the song "I Am a Muslim" from *We Are Muslim Children* by Saida Chaudry (ATP) about the most important Islamic duties. List the reasons given in the text for fasting. The class may add some new ones. Have the students draw pictures illustrating these reasons.

SACRIFICE

1. Describe with the help of the text how Muslims sacrifice animals as a part of the 'Id al-Adha celebration. Talk about how Muslims all over the world do so on that day. Discuss how the actual slaughter takes place. Some children may be troubled over the idea of killing an animal, so it would be wise to gather the students' views on this point, then discuss, explaining in simple terms that Allah permits killing only for food or self-protection, and then the killing must be done in a special way, especially seeing that the animal is treated as kindly as possible, and that the name of Allah is pronounced over it.

2. Explain why Muslims sacrifice an animal on 'Id al-Adha, and discuss other occasions like births, etc. when it is done. Read the children the story "Ibrahim's Son" for explanation and enrichment.

3. Discuss the meaning of sacrifice, first literally, as giving from the things we have received from Allah. Explain especially that Muslims do it for Allah, but the meat is given to the family, friends, relatives and poor people. Explain that the sacrifice on 'Id al-Adha is done for these reasons:

   - to show that Muslims obey Allah as Ibrahim did

   - to give up something they have for others

   - to remember the story of Ibrahim

4. Applying values: Talk about another meaning of the word sacrifice, which means giving up something a person likes or wants. The most familiar keyword familiar to the children is sharing. Ask the students to name some things that they have which they like very much. In a 5-minute exercise, let each child write or draw on a sheet or half-sheet of paper three important things from his/her possessions. Have each child name those things and tell how they could be shared, and with whom, (i.e., could the thing be cut into pieces to share, could it be given away to someone else, or could someone else borrow it? ; would it be shared with a parent, a brother or sister, a friend, or someone who is poor, either close to home or faraway?)

Activity: Make a list of different items that can be sacrificed/shared, such as THINGS, such as toys, clothing (especially when it is outgrown or when you have a lot), FOOD (shared with guests at home, with friends whenever you have it, or with hungry people), MONEY (discuss how parents spend for their children, how Muslims must spend for good things for others, and how every Muslim should give some of his/her money for charity), and finally TIME (this may be a novel concept for the children which needs some discussion. Ask the students how people can give up, or sacrifice time — helping someone, saying a kind word or giving hugs and love, and doing what people ask us to do, like when parents ask us to do chores at home, etc.

Finally, discuss the meaning of sacrifice as putting aside what we want sometimes, learning not to be selfish. Give an example of a younger child who wants a toy you are playing with. Talk about whether it is easy or difficult to forget that you want it and let the other child have it. Another example is sacrificing when you are angry. An example is when your brother, sister or parents do something that makes you upset or angry. When you sacrifice, you don't just think about how you want to yell and cry and hit someone; you think about how everyone will feel bad when you get angry, so you try to forgive them. Tell the children this is a kind of sacrifice that Allah loves very much. Sometimes it is very difficult, and people often forget, but they should keep trying and practice.

ROLE-PLAY (Charades): Have the children act out scenes of people sacrificing these things, and let their classmates guess what they are acting out.

PILGRIMAGE (HAJJ)

This segment of the text needs more additional explanation than the others, due to the background history involved and the amount of terminology associated with it. This lesson may be profitably combined with an Islamic studies unit on the topic, since it is impossible to provide all the necessary information here. The lesson should be built around the idea that the Hajj journey and the 'Id al-Adha celebration and the Hajj journey are about obeying Allah and remembering important events from long ago. The universal concept is that many celebrations in Islam and in other cultures are about remembering important events. By remembering the events, people remember the important ideas associated with them.

A. Ask the children to identify Prophet Ibrahim as the one of the most important prophets, the father of the prophets. You may write his name in Arabic on the chalkboard. Alternatively, the children may color the arabic outlines of Ibrahim and Ishmael's names from the Library of Islam publication *Color and Learn the Names of the Prophets* (by Hamza, 1989) on pages 12 and 13.

B. Call attention to the term Hajj. Write the word in Arabic on the chalkboard.

Describing the Hajj: Add information about the Hajj journey using sources, like

Aramco World Magazine, "Journey of a Lifetime" (July-August 1992) to show the worshippers and their activities on Hajj. Make a picture chart of what pilgrims do on Hajj. (See WORKSHEET #7) Locate Makkah on a map, and determine its location relative to the students' location. Talk about how a person could travel there (airplane, boat, car, etc.) Show pictures of the Kaaba and other places, and tell the stories behind them. Discuss the male pilgrims' appearance, all dressed alike in very simple clothing, and women's clothing, which is more variable, but which many women have made similar in simplicity to that required for men. No one can tell who is rich or poor, king or servant. Explain that this reminds Muslims that everyone is important to Allah, and that He wants everyone to believe in Him and serve Him together. Go over the chart, discussing the story behind each act, using the picture as a springboard to tell the enrichment story associated with it, located in this guide, pages 82 to 94.

Why Muslims make the Hajj journey: (See Enrichment activities, #2 in this Section) Use the chart again to discuss WHY Muslims make the Hajj journey. The first point there is "to worship Allah." Explain that worshipping means remembering, thinking about and praying to Allah. Once in their lives, Muslims try to visit the Kaaba in Makkah, the most special place for Muslims, for a very special worship. They ask Allah to forgive them, and they pray for His help. They feel very close to Allah at the Kaaba, because it is a very special house of worship that Allah ordered His prophet, Ibrahim to build. He built it with his son, Ismail, a long time ago. This information will introduce the series of stories retold briefly on the enrichment story pages 53 - 57, and told in the additional literature listed.

The importance of Hajj and 'Id al-Adha: A most important objective in discussing the background of Hajj for 'Id al-Adha is the concept of celebrations to remind people of stories from long ago, and of important people and places. As the stories are told to the children, show pictures of the places commemorated in the Hajj. Talk about each story and what are the important values, or things to remember, found in each. How does remembering these stories help people to be good and obey Allah?

Summarizing: Discuss with the students how it helps to think about things together so they are easier to remember. Talk about the importance of 'id for remembering and connecting with all Muslims past and present during the Hajj and 'id celebration. Emphasize that when Muslims celebrate 'Id al-Adha, they think about Ibrahim and his obedience. They remember the stories of Ibrahim and his family, especially when they sacrifice the animal and share its meat. Making Hajj is also about obedience to Allah, as one of the five pillars of Islam. Muslims think about their friends and family on Hajj, and it helps them about all the Muslims together all over the world. Similarly, fasting together makes it easier, and reminds people that all Muslims share this activity and sacrifice of comfort around the world, and reminds us that many people suffer hunger and thirst every day.

ACQUIRING SKILLS: Making a Hajj Picture Chart:

Use the pictures on Worksheet #7 to make a bulletin board display, or use the worksheet as an individual activity. Make a transparency of the worksheet as a classroom discussion aid. Have the students color the picture and write the name of each part of the Hajj on the line under the picture. They could then write each word on a separate sheet of paper and write or copy a sentence about what happens there (DRESSING IN IHRAM CLOTHES, GOING AROUND KAABA, DRINKING ZAMZAM WATER, GOING BETWEEN SAFA AND MARWA, THROWING STONES AT SHAITAN, STANDING AT ARAFAT, ETC.)

ACQUIRING SKILLS:

1. Find out from TV, radio, telephone weather report or newspaper what time sunrise and sunset occur. A very enterprising class might use old newspapers, or Islamic prayer time calendars to find out how the time differs from season to season throughout the year.

2. To explain the difference between dawn and sunrise, make the following demonstration. Use a darkened room, a globe and a flashlight to show how the sun's light is visible and lights up the sky before the sun can actually be seen. Explain that Muslims fast starting with the first light, not at sunrise. Show a sample of a Ramadan calendar showing the time chart for prayers and fasting.

3. Locate Makkah and Madinah on the globe or world map.

4. Use Worksheet #7 and the *Aramco World Magazine* article, "Journey of a Lifetime" (July-August 1992) or other source to describe the stations of the Hajj. Cut out the pilgrim figure and trace his route across the page, or trace his steps in pencil. Emphasize the need to make the visits in a certain order. Make sure he visits all the stations in order.

ENRICHMENT:

1. Teach the songs "'Id Ul-Fitr" and "I Travel to Mecca" from *We Are Muslim Children* by Saida Chaudry (ATP).

2. Stories for comprehension and enrichment, the text of which is found on the following four pages. Student versions of the stories are reproduced in Part IV of this binder.

- Allah is Greatest

- The Idols

- Ibrahim's Father

- Hajar and Her Baby

- Ibrahim's Son

- Building the Kaaba

Note: The first three stories of this group are taken from the Kindergarten Unit in this series of supplementary units. The others were prepared for this unit.

ALLAH IS GREATEST

The Qur'an tells the story of Ibrahim. Ibrahim was a very special young man. He worshiped Allah. His people worshiped idols. Ibrahim wanted to show his people that Allah is the Greatest. Allah showed him signs.

Ibrahim and his people looked up at the sky one night. They saw a beautiful star shining. Ibrahim said, "Could this be the Greatest? Could this be Allah?" But then, the star went out of sight. That couldn't be the Greatest!

Then they saw the moon come up in the sky. A bright, shining circle in the sky! "Could this be my Lord?" But then the moon set into the shadows, just like the star. He prayed that Allah would help them understand.

Then they saw the sun rise. The brightest light, like a fire lighting up the whole world! "Could this be my Lord? Could this be the Greatest?" But then, at the end of the day, the sun set. The light of the sun was gone. Darkness came again and his people saw the stars and the moon. They saw how they lit up the dark night. They saw the sun, the biggest thing in the sky. Sunshine made it warm and made everything grow.

But the stars, moon and sun went away. There must be something greater. Ibrahim knew that Allah, his Lord, made the stars, moon and sun. He made the land and the water. He made the trees and our food. He made all the animals and people. He made Ibrahim and his family. Allah made everything! Allah is the Greatest!

From Qur'an, 6:76-80

THE IDOLS

Ibrahim's family and their friends didn't believe in Allah. They didn't know what Allah helped Ibrahim to understand. They used to pray to idols. They had some that were shaped like animals. They had some shaped like people. Some looked like monsters.

They believed that these idols helped them. They thought the idols could make it rain or make the sun shine. If they were sick, they asked the idols to make them well. Sometimes they put food and drinks in front of them.

Ibrahim told the people to believe in Allah. He told them Allah is the greatest. He told them that Allah created everything. He told them to stop praying to idols. He told the people they were wrong.

Those people got very angry at Ibrahim. He was a young man telling them what to do. He said, "I believe Allah is the greatest. You will see that you are wrong."

When the people went away, Ibrahim went to the idols and broke them. He did not break the biggest one. The people called that one the chief idol.

The people saw their idols broken. They were angry and scared. They brought Ibrahim and asked him, "Who did this to our gods?"

Ibrahim was very clever. He said, "The chief idol did it. Ask the idols, if they can talk."

They answered, "You know they cannot talk!"

So Ibrahim asked, "Why do you pray to something that can't talk or even help itself?" "You pray to these instead of Allah. But they can't help you or hurt you."

But the people didn't like to hear that they were wrong. They tried to burn Ibrahim. But Allah saved him from their fire.

From Qur'an, 21:51-71

IBRAHIM'S FATHER

Ibrahim's father was named Azar. Ibrahim loved him and wanted to help him. He was an idol-maker. He also believed that the idols could help people or hurt them. Azar worshiped the idols.

Ibrahim asked his father, "Why do you worship idols? They can't see, they can't make themselves. They can't help you or hurt you."

His father was angry. Ibrahim said, "Believe in Allah. I know something that you don't know. Allah helped me to understand. Don't follow the Satan! I don't want Allah to punish you."

Ibrahim's father was so angry that he forgot himself. He told Ibrahim, "You don't believe in my gods?" He said, "I will stone you if you don't stop talking about Allah!" Ibrahim's father told him, "Go away from me for a long time!"

Was Ibrahim angry at his father? Did he try to hit him or say angry words back? No, Ibrahim was very sad. He wanted his father to believe in Allah. He wanted him to go to Paradise. Ibrahim asked Allah to forgive his father. He remembered his father's love and kindness when he was not angry.

From Qur'an, 6:75-80; 9:114; 19:41-48; 21:51-56; 26:77-86; 37:83-99

HAJAR AND HER BABY

Prophet Ibrahim had a wife named Sarah. They lived together for many years. They still had no children. Sarah loved her husband, and she wanted him to be happy. She told him he could marry Hajar, her servant girl. Prophet Ibrahim married her. Hajar had a son named Ismael. When Sarah saw the baby, she felt jealous. She told Ibrahim to take Hajar and her son away.

Ibrahim took Hajar and her baby to a place in the desert called Makkah. Allah told Ibrahim to leave his wife Hajar and the baby. He left them alone in a dry valley between the mountains. He left them with some water. He believed that Allah would care for them.

After a while, the waterskin was empty. Hajar and her baby Ismael were very thirsty. The baby cried. Hajar was afraid he would die. She went up one of the hills to look for signs of people. Perhaps some people would pass by and share their water. She came down and went up another hill to look. When she came back to Ismael, she found him almost dead. She went back and forth between the hills seven times. She was going back to her baby when she heard a voice. "Help us if you can," she said. It was the Angel Jibril's voice, sent by Allah! Jibril hit the earth with his heel. Water gushed out of the ground! Hajar was surprised. She began to dig in the ground. They drank and thanked Allah, who answered Hajar's prayer.

Hajar and Ismael stayed near the water. After a while, some people saw birds flying above the water. They came to Hajar and asked to stay with her. She told them the story. They put up their tents. They took care of Hajar and the baby.

The water that came to Hajar and Ismael is the well of Zamzam. After a long time, the well became covered up. Allah showed it to Prophet Muhammad's grandfather in a dream. He dug it up again. Since then, it has flowed. Pilgrims to Makkah still drink it today. Pilgrims walk where Hajar ran looking for water.

From Hadith Sahih Al Bukhari, 4:584

IBRAHIM'S SON

Ibrahim's son Ismael was very gentle and kind. Ibrahim loved him very much, as fathers love their children.

One night, Ibrahim had a dream. Ibrahim was a Prophet of Allah. Allah talks to Prophets in their dreams. So if Ibrahim saw something in a dream, he had to do that.

Ibrahim's dream told him to kill his son for Allah. The dream told him to sacrifice Ismael. Ibrahim knew he had to do it. He decided to talk to his son.

One day, Ibrahim and Ismael were walking together. Ibrahim told his son, "My dear son, I had a dream. I saw in the dream that I have to sacrifice you." He asked his son, "What do you think about that?"

Ismael loved his father very much. He also loved Allah. He knew that his father had to obey Allah. He had to do what Allah told him. So he was very brave. He told his father, "Oh, my father, do what Allah commands. I will bear it, if Allah wills."

Ibrahim got ready with the knife. Ismael put his face down. They believed in Allah very much. But it was very, very hard for them.

Then something happened. A voice called Ibrahim! The voice said, "Oh Ibrahim! You have already obeyed me! You have done what the dream told."

Then, as Ibrahim and Ismael watched in surprise, a huge ram, like a big sheep with horns appeared. It was suddenly in the place where Ismael lay down to be killed!

Father and son were very happy. They killed the ram instead of Ismael, and they had a lot of good meat.

Allah didn't want Ismael to die. He wanted to test them. He wanted to see if they would obey. Father and son obeyed Allah together. He gave them a good reward.

From Qur'an, 37:99-109

BUILDING THE KAABA

Prophet Ibrahim came to his son at Makkah, called Bakkah in those days. He and Ismael were thankful for Allah's mercy to their family. They built a house where people could worship Allah. They built it where Allah showed them.

Ibrahim and Ismael gathered stones from the mountains nearby. They dug in the earth to make the house stand firm. They cut and piled the stones. They put a special stone to mark one corner of the house. They built the four walls row by row. The walls rose higher. Ismael brought a rock for his father to stand on. Prophet Ibrahim stood on the rock to build the top of the walls.

Ibrahim and Ismael prayed to Allah while they built the Kaaba. They said, "Accept the work from us." He asked Allah to make them and their families Muslims and show them how to worship. He asked Allah to make them and their people into a nation who loves and obeys Allah. He asked Allah to send a prophet from Ismael's sons and grandchildren and teach the people . He said "Make this place safe and give its believing people fruits and riches!"

You can make pilgrimage, or Hajj. You can visit the Kaaba that Ibrahim and Ismael built. You can go around the house seven times as they did. You can stand to pray where Prophet Ibrahim and his son stood.

From Qur'an 2:125-127; 3:96-97; 14:37-41; Hadith Sahih Al Bukhari, 4:584

SECTION 4: HOW DO ALL MUSLIMS CELEBRATE EID?

PRE-READING:

Find out how many different countries are represented among the students. Explain that even though Muslims come from many different places, they celebrate 'id in much the same ways. Ask what takes place before and during the 'id celebration, or have them ask at home first. Compare answers before reading this section together.

COMPREHENSION / LEARNING NEW CONCEPTS:

1. Unity of all Muslims: Discuss things which ALL Muslims do, no matter where they are (Pray, say the same things like "bismillah" and "al-hamdu lillah" and "Assalaamu 'alaikum" as well as many du'a; they also make wudu' the same way, etc.). Several of the most important elements of Islam are that Muslims pray at the same times, in the same way; that they use greetings, du'a and prayers in Arabic, as well as reading Qur'an. Ask: "What is the last thing we do when we are finished with the prayer? (Turn our heads to the right and left and say "Salaamu 'alaikum wa rahmat Allahi wa barakatuhu.") Discuss why Muslims do this, (to think about Muslims everywhere). State that celebration of 'id is another way that Muslims think about each other in the family, the community and around the world.

2. Celebration demonstrates Islamic values: Discuss preparations for a celebration. Are these things people do all the time? (like cleaning, cooking, bathing, dressing) How do these preparations differ for 'id? (they are done especially well or they are done in special ways for a festival) Why is it important to do each of these things anytime, but especially for a celebration? Tell the students how looking at what people do for a celebration, tells us what is important to them all the time. Explain that important things people like to do are called VALUES. Ask the students to name the preparations and activities for 'id, and make a list on the board, illustrating each activity with a picture. After each item, place an arrow. Ask the students what is important about doing these things, or why are they done.

ACTIVITY	ISLAMIC VALUES
cleaning house, taking baths, new clothes	→ cleanliness and neatness
cooking and cleaning	→ working together
making special food for guests, sharing meat	→ enjoying and sharing Allah's gifts
giving gifts to friends and poor people	→ being generous
going to 'id prayer all together	→ joining together to worship
greeting and visiting	→ keeping good relations with people
listening to Qur'an, talk about Ibrahim, etc.	→ remembering important things together

One of the most important values is including everyone, young and old, rich and poor, families, friends and people we don't know. Discuss the idea that a Muslim who stays by himself and does not meet with others is easy prey for the Shaitan (See Wolf and Sheep Metaphor). Show students the literal meaning of the metaphor by using pictures or drawings, or using a version of Aesop's Fables on the subject of the Wolf and the Sheep. Then apply the meaning in the context of Islam. When people celebrate, they take a break from busy lives, meet people they have not seen for a while, and find out how they are. Poor people are taken care of, and everyone has a good time together, at least twice a year. Of course, Muslims should do this all the time, but as the lesson indicated, celebrations show what people should do all year 'round, but on 'id, they do it even more.

ACQUIRING SKILLS/ENRICHMENT:

These projects add atmosphere and excitement to the unit. They work best if the unit is timed to coincide with the actual 'id celebration.

1. Cooking:

    a. Make a cookbook/recipe booklet for the parents by asking each child's parents to write down a favorite recipe for 'id sweets. Teacher and/or parent helpers good at word processing can type the recipes, one to a page. Have each child make small drawings or borders to decorate their family's recipe page. Collect, copy and staple together individual booklets for each member of the class. Finally, make a cover decorated with paint, crayons or collage materials.

    b. Cooking demonstration: Have a parent, older sibling in the school, or professional chef from the community visit to demonstrate a special recipe. Alternatively, the teacher may make sweets with the class. Most important is student participation in the process, which becomes a math and science lesson when students help to mix and measure. It might be fun to videotape the session and play it back like the TV cooking programs. Another interesting angle for development of thinking skills involves deciding what steps to show the viewer and how to best demonstrate the process. For example, have the students decide what comes first, next, last, etc.

2. Making 'id cards:

    A variety of media can be used to make 'id greeting cards, such as printing with felt, sponges, objects, leaves, etc., painting or collage. In the proper season, the cards could be decorated with pressed flowers or leaves, turning the process into a science lesson as natural materials are gathered, examined and pressed. Library books on the subject suggest simple methods. The message should include Arabic script, so that a number of alternatives for learning activities are also possible here. The Arabic teacher might work with the class to develop a message, use the variations in Worksheets #3 and 4 to copy, color in or cut out and paste into their cards.

Important is learning what is traditionally said in greeting for 'id, how it is written and what it means.

The number of cards made by each child depends on the medium used, and students may exchange cards with classmates, take them home to parents or send them to students in another class. Alternatively, make an activity of addressing, stamping and mailing them to another Muslim school, or to friends and relatives elsewhere. This would provide a tie-in to communications lessons.

3. Collecting food or money for the poor:

    Have each student bring in canned goods or similar durably packaged, non-spoiling groceries. Money can be collected in an empty ring-top soda can, or in a box which has been taped shut and slit at the top. Each child can take the can home, for example at the beginning of Ramadan, to receive pocket change, etc.until the end of the month. Before the collection is undertaken, discuss with the students how the class might find out where there are needy people who could receive a gift of food, or how a donation of money might be put to good use. Parents or the teacher may help in providing a link to community workers who have such information. Such a worker could be a guest speaker. The students would then participate in planning how the collected food or money will reach the people for whom it is intended.

SECTION 5: WHAT ARE SOME EID CUSTOMS AROUND THE WORLD?

SECTION PRE-READING:

1. Show a globe or map of the world. Show how the land is divided into many countries. Muslims live in nearly every country in the world. Ask students to name the country of their parents' or their own birth. Explain that in some countries, almost everyone is Muslim. In other countries, some or only a few of the people are Muslim. Give examples. Are there many Muslims in the country where you are?

2. Review the idea in Section 4 that all Muslims do certain things on 'id. Ask for examples.

3. Explain that each country also has special things that they do which are different from other countries.

4. Since only ten countries are discussed here, more comprehensive coverage can be obtained by asking students to fill in information with research from their own families. Students may collect information, photos, draw pictures and interview family members to make a display of customs from their own countries, regions or families. Experience with this unit has shown that children whose countries are not named here felt somewhat left out. This activity more than compensates.

PAKISTAN: Watching for the moon

PRE-READING:

1. Point to Pakistan on a map or globe. Identify the continent of Asia.

2. Introduce the concept of a "Muslim country" in simple terms, building on the Section pre-reading, above.

COMPREHENSION:

3. Show pictures of hills, mountains and valleys, high land and low land from library books or scenic calendars (the latter suggests a bulletin board display). Identify Pakistan as a land with hills, valleys and very high mountains. A relief map or globe will also show that Pakistan has very high land and very low land, and a large river. A related comprehension/enrichment activity is passing out playdough or other clay on cardboard or styrofoam trays for the students to model mountains and flat land. Use a pencil to scratch in a river.

LEARNING NEW CONCEPTS / ACQUIRING SKILLS :

4. Review the Section 1 lesson on the Islamic calendar and phases of the moon or implement it at this time. Note that people wait for the end of the month of Ramadan by watching the moon. Explain that all the Muslims stop fasting and have 'id when someone, somewhere sees the new moon. When the last sliver of moon disappears, they know the time is near. Then, they watch on the roofs for the new crescent to appear.

5. Different lands, different conditions, different ways to get information: Ask: Have you ever seen the moon and stars from where you live? Have them observe the sky at night as a homework project and report on what they saw (they may write a sentence or two or draw a picture of what they saw). Discuss the findings, also utilizing students' memories of seeing stars at home or in other countries. Why can't we see the moon everywhere by the eye alone (clouds, city lights, trees, etc.)? How can Muslims find out about 'id if they can't see the moon where they live? Explain that in the desert and the mountains, far from city lights, people can see it best. They also ask scientists with big telescopes to look for the new moon. When someone sees it, they can quickly tell other Muslims around the world by telephone, radio, or TV.

ENRICHMENT:

6. Plan a field trip to a planetarium, or have a guest speaker interested in astronomy show the students a telescope or a filmstrip or video suitable to the age group.

7. Look up information about the moon in an encyclopedia or other fact book appropriate to the students' abilities. Learn how the moon revolves around the earth, how the earth casts its shadow to produce the different shapes, etc.

8. Moon and stars picture: Use black construction paper, glue and silver or gold glitter to make stars and a crescent moon. Using white school glue in an applicator, or with a brush, make a large crescent in the middle of the paper. Make a number of stars on the rest of the paper. Shake glitter over the wet glue, then shake off the excess onto a newspaper. Hang picture to dry thoroughly before handling. Alternate method: Outline a crescent moon and stars on a piece of black construction paper. Cut or punch out the shapes carefully. Mount the black sky over a piece of silver or gold wrapping paper or aluminum foil. Yellow or white tissue paper can be used as well, and can be hung in a window for light to shine through.

IRAN: Putting new shoes under their pillow

PRE-READING:

1. Point to Iran on a map or globe. Identify the continent of Asia.

2. Note that Iran is also a "Muslim country."

COMPREHENSION:

3. Point out the masjid shown in the window of the illustration. Explain that if you lived in Iran, you might have such a building in your neighborhood. Explain that in countries where many Muslims live, every neighborhood has one or more masjid. Compare/contrast with the situation in your local area.

4. Review Section 3, "Getting Ready," for universal 'id customs. Remind them that everywhere, Muslim parents try to get new clothes and shoes for their children for 'id, or prepare their children's best clothing. Ask for students' ideas on why the Iranian children might put their shoes under their pillows. Note that in some places, this is the only time of the year when children receive new shoes, because their parents cannot afford many new things for family members. Thus, new shoes are something very special. How do you feel when you get shiny, new shoes? What are your favorite kind of new shoes?

LEARNING NEW CONCEPTS:

5. Children everywhere are special gifts from Allah: Discuss with the class how Islam teaches love and care for children, and how 'id is also a very special time for them. Draw pictures of the children's favorite part of 'id celebration. For stories on love for children in Islam, see *Love At Home*, *A Great Friend of Children*, and *Muslim Nursery Rhymes* (Islamic Foundation Publications).

6. Explain that in many lands (and cultures), customs show how people love children and give them many things, besides caring for them every day. Think of some customs that are fun for children, both in your country and in other lands. (Examples: amusement parks, gifts and new clothes for 'id, playgrounds, birthday parties, trick or treat, puppet shows, songs, holiday games, etc.) The class may enjoy doing some research on children's customs in a picture book library.

ENRICHMENT:

7. Show photographs of masjid from Iran. Discuss the colored tiles used to make the beautiful designs inside and out.

8. Make paper mosaics using glue and small bits of colored paper.

EGYPT: Ramadan lanterns

PRE-READING:

1. Point to Egypt on a map or globe. Identify the continent of Africa

2. Note that Egypt is a "Muslim country."

COMPREHENSION:

3. Identify the Nile River mentioned in the text. Have students trace it with their finger on a map, and tell the countries it flows through. Ask the students how the text describes Egypt (hot and dry, and having many people). Explain that the river is very important for Egypt because of the weather, and to help grow food and to have water for all the people.

4. Using the text and illustration, have the students discuss the custom described. In the evening, groups of three or four children go out into the streets in a parade, swinging their glowing lanterns and singing an old Ramadan song. There is a whole street in Cairo which is filled with lantern shops during Ramadan, from very large ones for homes and hotels to small ones for children. They are made from colored glass and shiny metal, often cut from old tin cans. Additional background information on this custom can be found in *Aramco World Magazine* (March-April 1992) or by asking the parent of an Egyptian student.

LEARNING NEW CONCEPTS:

5. Doing special things that are fun: Explain that many countries have customs which are fun for children. What holiday customs do you know about from other cultures and countries? The teacher may help out here with familiar customs or library books. (Trick or Treat, Maypoles, parades, making ornaments for Christmas trees, decorating eggs, origami toys and decorations for holidays in China and Japan, paper cutouts all over the world, dances and puppet or shadow-puppet shows in Indonesia etc.). Discuss the meaning of these customs, like eggs in spring celebrations for new growth, origami birds as symbols of hope, peace and happiness, etc. Discuss the meaning of the Ramadan lanterns, especially about the meaning of light in Islam, as in the light of Qur'an, the truth as light and ignorance as darkness, especially the beauty of light in the colored lanterns, and lights used to decorate the house on 'id. The custom also shows how Muslim peoples love children, since the children bring light and beauty and song and happiness into the houses of their families and all people. In almost all Muslim countries, 'id day is a time of special fun for children, with donkey, elephant and camel rides, big swings set up in town and village squares with other carnival rides.

ACQUIRING SKILLS:

6. Using pictures to tell about geography: This activity applies to several countries mentioned in the unit. Obtain library picture books about the Muslim world. Show the students a variety of photos of Muslim countries. Have the students identify visual clues which tell about the geography of a place, like the kind of scenery shown, or the kind of things that grow there, or the clothing worn by people outdoors. Is the land high or low? Is it hot or cold? Is it dry or rainy? If possible, show some pictures taken in different seasons, like during the dry and wet seasons in India or Africa, in summer and winter elsewhere, etc. Explain also that some countries don't have very different seasons, like some tropical ones, where it is hot and rainy most of the time.

ENRICHMENT:

7. Making Ramadan lanterns: There are several ways to make lanterns similar to the ones used in Egypt, both 2- and 3-dimensional. The simplest method is to cut out a frame of cardboard or construction paper in the shape of a lantern, decorate it with crayons, glitter, silver paper or paint, then add colored tissue paper or colored cellophane (acetate) glued into the frame for the "lamp". The finished lantern can be hung in a window. The second method is to fold a piece of construction paper crosswise into four sections, cutting a rectangular or fancy-shaped hole in each panel. Glue a piece of tissue paper or acetate on the back, fold into a square tube, and attach a strip of paper at the top for a handle. A third method is to use paper milk cartons, oatmeal boxes, or other types of cartons, making a design for the light to shine through by cutting out shapes, piercing the carton with a pencil or scissor point to make a design. Glue colored cellophane or tissue paper behind the cut-outs and attach a string or cardboard strip for a handle. Put a small flashlight inside the finished lantern. For classroom display, hang the lanterns on a string of colored electric party lights along a wall or window.

NEVER USE CANDLES : FIRE HAZARD!

TURKEY: Ramadan drummer

PRE-READING:

1. Point to Turkey on a map or globe. Identify the continents of Europe and Asia.

2. Note that Turkey is a "Muslim country."

COMPREHENSION:

3. Identify Turkey on a relief globe or map, letting students trace the seacoast and feel the mountains with their finger. Point out some cities and tell them that other areas have farms where people grow crops to eat or sell.

4. Discuss why the drummer is important during Ramadan, when he comes, and why the people want to wake up early, eat and pray. Review the text from Sections 1 and 2 if needed.

LEARNING NEW CONCEPTS:

5. Helping each other to be good Muslims: Discuss how the Ramadan drummer, who is found in many Muslim countries (some use a different instrument), helps Muslims to follow Islam (He helps them to wake up for an early meal so they can keep on fasting; he helps everyone get up in time for prayer.). Think of other ways in which Muslims help each other to follow what Allah wants them to do. Make a list or draw pictures which represent these ways.

6. Kinds of local communication: How do Muslims get up to pray the dawn prayer when it is not Ramadan (they hear adhan from masjid or radio)? Discuss with the class how the adhan and the drummer represent a special kind of communication. How far away could a drum be heard? What other kinds of local communication can be used to carry messages a short distance? Contrast the kind of communication which requires many people (person-to-person talking and telephoning). Which kinds can be heard by many people at once (using microphone, a person with a loud voice, whistles, horns, and drums, radio and TV)? Which ones communicate both near and far? Which kinds need a long time (books and newspapers, letters), and which ones are very fast (voice, drum, caller, electronic media)?

ACQUIRING SKILLS:

7. Communicating without words: Ask students to think of other ways people communicate without words, and discuss when these kinds of communication are used. Some examples are hand and light signals and horn honking in traffic, sign language for hearing impaired, whistles for sports coaches, buzzers and bells in school and telephones, appliances and fire alarms. The teacher may add some examples from science (light and mirror signaling, morse code) and history/culture (town criers,

gongs, trumpets, smoke signals, and African and native American drums). As an activity, invent and practice using aural signals to communicate in the classroom.

ENRICHMENT:

8.   Drums, drums, drums: Find out other ways people around the world have used drums to communicate. Obtain library books on drums and their uses, or invite an African, native American or other guest speaker to demonstrate different types of drums and their uses. For science crossover, find out why different sized and shaped drums make different sounds.

HOLLAND: Ramadan box

PRE-READING:

1. Point to Holland on a map or globe. Identify the continent of Europe.

2. Note that Muslims live in Holland, but it is not a Muslim country.

COMPREHENSION:

3. Discuss the term "few Muslims."   How much is "many" and how much is "few"? The class will probably agree that few refers to the number of people in the country who are Muslim, while most people are not Muslims in Holland. Test the idea by comparison with the local area.

4. Why do the Muslims in Holland have a Muslim school? How is their school probably like yours?

5. Demonstrate the idea of the sharing box by asking everyone to put a different object in a box and then have each student take out one object. This is an interesting idea for use in other classroom activities, such as spelling drills, math problems, sharing artwork, etc.

LEARNING NEW CONCEPTS/ACQUIRING SKILLS:

6. The focus in this segment is on the concept of cooperating in areas where there are, comparatively, not many Muslims. To introduce this highly abstract and relative idea, ask the students whether there are many or not many Muslims in their local community, school or neighborhood. Discuss, compare and evaluate the answers, which will probably reflect some uncertainty as to the meaning of "many" and "few". The following activities will help to clarify the concept.

7. The many/few idea can be tested with various colored beans or beads in a jar. Choose contrasting colors. Start a heap of one color beans in a plastic tub. Ask the students with each addition whether they think there are many or few. When they say "yes", then put the beans in another tub with a substantially larger number of contrasting colored beans. Ask the students if the first color still seems to be many or few.

8. To apply the concept, ask which students have visited the masjid or attended 'id prayers outdoors. Ask whether there seem to be a lot of Muslims there at one time. Contrast this with, for example, the number of Muslims who are neighbors to each child. Explain that in some places, most of the people are not Muslim. When they all collect together and cooperate, they seem like many. When they stay apart without cooperating, they seem fewer.

9. Discuss the term cooperate. In what ways do Muslims cooperate? Muslims meet together to share work, learning, prayers and celebrations. Apply these concepts to circumstances in your local community.

ENRICHMENT:

10. Find out or estimate how many Muslims live in your community. What is the total population of your city or town?

11. Consult a chart of world population data with the teachers' help, and find out which countries have the most and fewest Muslims in their population.

12. To make a graphic comparison of the number of Muslims in the total world population, choose similar sized beans in two different colors. Measure out 4 cups of one color, and one cup of the other. Show them first as five separate heaps on a table. Then combine the four cups and place this next to the one cup. Finally, you may wish to mix the two types, showing how Muslims live all over the world.

13. Discuss several quotes from Qur'an, such as Surat al-Nasr, which talk about large numbers of people entering Islam, and explain how Islam is the religion which Allah wants for everyone to live peacefully together on earth. Explain that Muslims' duty is to tell people about Islam, but especially, to be a good example for others to follow. If Muslims act as Allah wanted, others will want to be Muslims, too.

14. Making a Ramadan Calendar: A familiar custom in Europe is Advent calendars for children. This custom can be usefully and simply adapted to the Islamic month of Ramadan, especially as a means for encouraging children to try fasting for a number of days at least. The basic method for the calendar is a grid of 29 numbered, small containers into which a piece of candy or a small toy is placed, one for each day, arranged like a calendar and decorated with Qur'an verses and colorful Islamic designs. Almost anything can be used as a basis, such as egg cartons stapled face down onto a poster board, with small, numbered doors cut out of the poster board to allow entry to the sections. A permanent calendar can be made from a piece of fabric with 29 numbered pockets sewn on. The simplest method involves stapling or gluing 29 numbered envelopes onto a poster or piece of butcher paper. For use in a classroom, a large piece of paper or a bulletin board can be used as the base, with 29 numbered, small paper lunch bags stapled or tacked on in a grid. These bags can hold enough small treats or toys for a whole class.

The calendar can be used in a variety of ways:

1. For younger children who don't yet fast, the calendar can be used to mark the days of Ramadan. Each day, 1 door is opened to reveal the treat, and the door is left open, marked or taken down.

2. For children who fast some or all of the days, the calendar is used to mark the passing of each day, but also to encourage and record the days actually fasted by the child. All the days contain a small treat to be enjoyed with iftar each day. But for each day the child fasts, the parent places a special treat or toy inside the door of the calendar for that day. At the end of the month, on the day of 'Id al-Fitr the sections are emptied and the number of days fasted is counted.

USA: Picnics in the park

PRE-READING:

1. Point to the United States on a map or globe. Identify the continent of North America.

2. Note that many Muslims live in the United States, but it is not a Muslim country.

COMPREHENSION:

3. Using the map, discuss what is meant in the text by the description "large country." Compare the size of the United States with that of other countries.

4. Ask the students to relate this American custom in their own words. Elicit their own experiences of fun after the prayer on the day of 'id.

LEARNING NEW CONCEPTS:

5. People on the move: Using the text's description of the U.S. as a place where many Muslims live, explain that many Muslims from all over the world live there, but most of the people in the U.S. are not Muslims. Review the concept of "few and many" from the lesson on Holland. Give reasons why people travel to the U.S., giving examples of countries from which they come. Explain, reviewing information from a social studies textbook about America as a land of mixed peoples. Some examples are the following:

   - people travel to take jobs

   - people travel to study in universities

   - people travel to learn about new places and things

   - people travel to visit relatives

   - people travel to see doctors and hospitals when they are very sick

   - people travel for fun

   - people travel to tell others about Islam

6. Muslims from many lands share in celebration: Ask what languages are spoken in the students' homes (English, Arabic, Urdu, Farsi, etc.). Explain that people from many different countries, such as Muslims in the U.S., speak many different languages and have many different customs. Sometimes they come together and invent a new custom that everyone can enjoy. Muslims in the U.S., for example, started meeting in parks on 'id for fun that everyone can understand and enjoy. In bad weather, they meet at masjid or other large indoor places like schools and community centers. As the text suggests, they have picnics or potlucks where everyone brings food from their own country. American Muslims cook American food, too. They

bring balloons, carnival rides and pony rides for all the children. Mention that the Muslims have carried this custom from their home countries, where elephant, camel and donkey rides, huge swings and ferris wheels are common 'id entertainments. Compare and contrast this with other customs they have read about.

ACQUIRING SKILLS / ENRICHMENT:

7. Gathering data and transferring it to a map: In classroom settings of mixed ethnic and national origin, especially in North America and Europe, students can make a bulletin board display showing the students' origin. Poll the class, or the school if practical, finding out the name of each student's country. Record each name with the country on a separate slip of paper. Have the students sort the paper slips, finding out how many different countries and how many in each country. Record the information on a large sheet of paper with two columns, one headed "Country", the other headed, "Number of Students." Transfer the information to a simple world map, using push pins or numbered flags on each country to show the number of students in the boundaries of each country represented. A simple bar graph could be made by entering the name and country on equal-sized cards or papers and mounting these in vertical or horizontal rows beside the country name. Further activities with the finished display involve naming the continents, finding out which continent and country has the most students.

TRINIDAD: Sharing 'id celebration with neighbors

PRE-READING:

1. Point to Trinidad on a map or globe. Identify the continent of South America. You may wish to identify the Caribbean Sea.

2. Remind the students of countries like the United States and Holland where some Muslims live, but many people there are not Muslim. Tell the students that in Trinidad, Muslims also live together with other groups. Trinidad is not a Muslim country.

COMPREHENSION / LEARNING NEW CONCEPTS:

3. Review or introduce the term ISLAND. Explain that there are many small and large islands in the oceans. Have individual students point out large and small islands on a globe or map. Explain that in the sea between N. and S. America, there are many beautiful islands. If the students are familiar with Christopher Columbus, tell them that he visited these islands in his ships.

4. Discuss the concept that Muslims in Trinidad have come from various places. Contrast this with some of the countries already discussed, like Turkey, Pakistan, Egypt and China, for example. Discuss what is meant by the statement that the grandfathers of Trinidad's Muslims came from India or Africa. Point out these places on a map or globe, showing how far it is to Trinidad. Rather than attempting to discuss the history involved, according to which Africans were brought there first (in the 1700's) as slaves on sugar plantations, while Indians came as indentured servants (about 150 years ago), you may prefer to use the childrens' families as examples. Where do their grandparents live? Where are they from? In countries like the U.S., many of the people have grandparents from a different country. Explain that a long time ago, people came in ships. How do they come nowadays? (in airplanes) Some students may be able to point out on a map their parents' or grandparents' place of origin.

5. Building on the first part of the lesson, discuss how Trinidad, like the U.S., is a place where people are mixed by the color of their skin, country of origin and religion. Discuss how all live together as neighbors. The most important concept in this lesson is about Islamic behavior toward neighbors. Discuss the fact that in Trinidad, everyone shares each other's celebrations, sharing customs, greetings and food. On 'id, television neighbors celebrate, bringing special programs from all over the Muslim countries of the world. Draw the parallel that television makes everyone around the world into neighbors.

   PROJECT: The class might have a project to prepare sweets or greeting cards to distribute to neighbors, either of individual students or of the school.

ENRICHMENT:

6. Read and discuss Hadith about how Muslims should treat neighbors of all faiths. Examples are found in *Stories of the Sirah*, Part VII (IQRA Publications, 1988), and *True Stories for Children* (TaHa Publications, 1993), and *Love Your Brother, Love Your Neighbor* (Islamic Foundation, 1983).

7. Read *My Little Island* by Frane' Lessac (Lippincott, 1984) a book about a small island in the Caribbean. The short, wonderful story about a visit to an island in the Caribbean, illustrated with naive paintings, was featured on PBS's "Reading Rainbow."

MALAYSIA: Cooking rice over an open fire

PRE-READING:

1. Point to Malaysia on a map or globe. Identify the continent of Asia.

2. Note that Malaysia is a "Muslim country".

COMPREHENSION:

3. Have a student locate Malaysia on the Poster Map. Name the continent.

4. Using the text, have students help to define the word peninsula. Contrast with island. Note that part of Malaysia is on a peninsula, and part on the island of Borneo, shared with another Muslim country, Indonesia.

5. Discuss the custom described in the text, explaining any unfamiliar terms, like "stalk," meaning the thick stem of the plant, which in the case of bamboo can be quite large, and hollow, with dividing sections at intervals along the stalk. This stalk would be cut just below the divider, leaving the top open, where a hole is drilled for hanging. The resulting "cup" is filled with sticky rice and sugar and baked slowly over the fire. Many of these "cups" are strung on a pole over the fire. Additional background information includes the following: Almost everyone celebrates 'id in the villages; as in many Muslim countries, the cities are emptied just before 'id. People must visit their grandparents or other relatives in their home villages. This is very exciting for children from the city, because they get to see farm animals, run in the fresh air, and meet their relatives. For village children, it means seeing cousins, aunts and uncles, and having lots of friends to play with. Visitors also mean toys, clothes and treats from the city. For everyone, it means good food and lots of fun! Relatives work together to cook and prepare special food, and serve all the guests.

LEARNING NEW CONCEPTS:

6. City/ Village (rural-urban): Review or introduce the differences between a village and a city. Discuss the following aspects —

    *   how the two places differ in the way they look (amount of trees, kind of streets and buildings)

    *   how they differ in the way people get their food (farm vs. store)

    *   how people's jobs and activities are different in each place (many jobs vs. limited jobs)

    *   how people communicate (basically the same nowadays)

    The last point can be used to discuss the links between city and village, such as bringing food in trucks, bringing supplies from city to village, city people go to village to visit, call on telephone, watch TV and listen to radio. The class can make a picture/word chart of links from village to city, from city to village, and both ways. Illustrate the chart with magazine pictures or student drawings. The chart below is only one example of how this might be done:

CITY		VILLAGE
canned food from factory	↔	fresh food from farm
people need food	↔	farmers need tools
people call on telephone	↔	people call on telephone
stations send TV/radio	↔	people use TV/radio
people visit	↔	people visit

7. Resources from near and far: Identify the items needed to make this traditional Malaysian 'id recipe (coconuts, rice and bamboo). Ask the students where the Malaysians get these items (The text states that they grow in Malaysia.). Tell the students that the things that grow or are found in a place are called RESOURCES. Tell or ask what resources are used for (food, clothes, houses, transportation and other things we use. Use the illustration to name some of the resources found in Malaysia (palm trees, rice, bamboo, wood for houses and firewood, etc.) For enrichment and practice, you may use some of the other illustrations to name resources in other places mentioned in this unit.

Explain that we use resources from near where we live, and from far away. Ask: Could we get the ingredients for this Malaysian dish where we live? How would we get them? Could we find some (coconut and rice in the store), but maybe not others (bamboo stalks, firewood)? How do these things come to us from faraway? (in airplanes, ships and trucks).

For enrichment and practice, identify some of the resources used for things in the classroom, or resources used to make their breakfast or lunch, and think about whether they come from near or far, and what kinds of transportation are used.

ACQUIRING SKILLS / ENRICHMENT:

8. Using pictures to tell about geography: This activity can be applied to several of the countries mentioned here. Egypt, for example, can be used for contrast. Obtain library books about the Muslim world that contain many photographs. Show a variety of scenes from Muslim countries. Have the students identify visual clues which tell about the geography of a place, like the kind of scenery shown, or the kind of things that grow there, or the clothing worn by people outdoors. Is the land high or low? Is it hot or cold? Is it dry or rainy? If possible, show some pictures taken in different seasons, like during the dry and wet seasons in India or Africa, in summer and winter elsewhere, etc. Explain also that some countries don't have very different seasons, like some tropical ones, where it is hot and rainy most of the time.

CHINA: Bread with a story

PRE-READING:

1. Point to China on a map or globe. Identify the continent of Asia.

2. Note that China is not a Muslim country, though many Muslims live there.

COMPREHENSION:

3. Discuss the description of China as "a very large country" with "more people than any other country." Look up China's exact population in an Atlas, or compare China's population with total world population. Use beans of different colors, or colored counters from math skills manipulative kits (Show a ratio of 4 parts to 1 part, for a total of 5 parts, each representing 1 billion people. The teacher may discuss or omit the concept of a billion.). Finally, explain that most Chinese are not Muslims, but there are still many Muslims in China.

4. As background to this Chinese Muslim custom, explain that this bread is always made at the time of 'id, and is recognized as a Muslim specialty. Explain the illustration by telling the class that the people who make this bread are poor people who have no other houses, so they live in the masjid, often young working men. Muslim families buy oil and flour, or give the money to buy oil and flour, and sometimes sugar, to these people in the masjid. They make the bread in the courtyard, or paved space behind the masjid, cooking it in oil, in large, round frying pans sitting on a stand. When finished, the bread is placed in bags for families to take home.

LEARNING NEW CONCEPTS / ACQUIRING SKILLS:

5. Stories tell about important values: To help the students understand the story behind the bread, tell them that it is from Hadith, or sayings and true stories told by Prophet Muhammad's companions. Explain that these Hadith stories are very important to Muslims, because they teach how Muslims should behave. In fact, they are almost as important as the Qur'an. Ask a student to retell the story for comprehension.

   Story cut-ups — Finding meaning in a story: As a small-group activity, make a photocopy of the story on page #42, beginning, "A poor woman..." and ending with "...thanked her and blessed her," using Worksheet #8. Cut the story into sentence strips as follows:

   A poor woman made bread for the Prophet.

   She had only a little flour.
   She had only a little oil.

The Prophet tasted the woman's bread.
The bread tasted very good.

It tasted good because the poor woman loved the Prophet.
Prophet Muhammad thanked and blessed her.

Divide the class into four groups, pairing readers and non-readers if necessary. Give each group a piece of the story. Modeling the activity using the first sentence, show them how to talk about it, asking: What does the sentence mean? Why it is important? What does the sentence tell about how Muslims should behave? Walk around the class, coaching the groups as necessary. Let each group present their conclusions after sufficient time for discussion (5 minutes or less). Use these findings to summarize the rich meanings and values in this story, as in the following examples:

- Being generous, especially to the Prophet

- Making an effort even when you don't have much.

- Accepting presents, even if they are not big and expensive

- Being happy with simple things

- Putting love into everything we do makes it better

- Always saying "thank you"

- Remembering the poor

- Honoring Prophet Muhammad ﷺ

Conclude why the Chinese or any other Muslims like to remember this story on 'id. Discuss why special days are a good time to remember and tell stories.

ENRICHMENT:

6. Read a selection of other stories which have important meanings. Use some selections from the Kindergarten unit in this series, "I Am a Muslim," in which hadith that feature the sahaba as children are presented along with companion stories about modern children and lesson activities. Other useful selections for enrichment include children's Islamic stories from the Islamic Foundation and the Stories of the Sirah collection by Tasneema and Abidullah Ghazi (IQRA Foundation). To provide enrichment from non-Islamic sources, Aesop's Fables or similar selections from other cultures and literatures may be used.

GAMBIA: Big families celebrate together

PRE-READING:

1. Point to the Gambia on a map or globe. Identify the continent of Africa.

2. Note that the Gambia is a "Muslim country."

COMPREHENSION:

3. Ask the children to describe the shape of the Gambia on the map, and find the river in the middle of it. Identify Senegal, which surrounds the Gambia. Have them point to the ocean.

LEARNING NEW CONCEPTS / ACQUIRING SKILLS:

4. Gambian Village Layout: Using Worksheet # 9A, provide background information about family compounds in Gambian villages, explaining that family compounds are found many African countries. Ask the students to count and describe the shape of the compounds and various houses in them, find the masjid, marketplace, well and the large tree where people of the village, particularly older men, meet together. Under the tree are mats or wooden seats. Why is a tree such a good gathering place? (It provides cool shade in a hot country, and it can symbolize tradition, since trees live for a long time.) Note the roads leading to the city, the fields for crops, the forest, and neighboring village. Discuss the two different kinds of houses, the square or rectangular ones being a newer type while the round type is older, or traditional. The round ones have thatched grass roofs, and have mud walls. The square or rectangular houses are sometimes brick, but may also be mud, and they often have roofs of metal, while some have thatch. Why is each compound fenced in (each contains a family group, with wives and sons and their children living together in separate houses and sharing more closely)? Note that the home of the village leader's home opens to the central area of the village, while the other houses are within the compound. Why is that (so he can receive visitors and others who need his help)? Discuss why large families like to live together (sharing work, helping with the children, protecting each other, sharing food, water and other resources and skills, having fun together). Note that the marketplace might contain small craft or repair shops, and that the masjid might be a fenced, open place or a more elaborate building with minarets and solid walls. Have students answer the questions on Worksheet #9B and color the features accordingly.

5. Use text, paragraphs 3 and 4 to explain how everyone in the family group has jobs. They cooperate every day to make their living, and especially on 'id. Ask the students to name the jobs for the family members mentioned in the text. Review information on the sacrifice of 'Id al-Adha from Section 3: Describe with the help of the text how Muslims sacrifice animals as a part of the 'Id al-Adha celebration. Talk about how people on Hajj in Mekkah do so and how Muslims all over the world

join them on that day. Discuss how the actual slaughter takes place. Some children may be troubled over the idea of killing an animal, so it would be wise to gather the students' views on this point, then discuss, explaining in simple terms that Allah permits killing only for food or self-protection, and then the killing must be done in a special way, in which the name of Allah is pronounced before the animal is killed.

6. Using the illustration and paragraphs 3 and 4, compare and contrast the 'id dinner in Gambia with the customs in other lands described, like the United States, Malaysia and the illustration of baking in Section 3, as well as with their own family's 'id dinner. Pay particular attention to the way the family sits (on the ground, on low stools, at chairs and table), the type of pots and dishes used, and what kind of utensils are used for eating (fingers, gourd spoons, chopsticks, metal spoons, knives and forks). Explain that the way people eat is also a custom. The teacher may mention that Prophet Muhammad 🕌 liked to sit on the ground or floor, and eat with his right hand. Because Muslims follow his example, this is an Islamic custom for eating.

ENRICHMENT:

7. Trying out different ways of eating: Make a tray of different types of food, and experiment with different ways of eating, using fingers, gourd spoons, wooden spoons, chopsticks and a selection of fancy forks and spoons of different types from Western "silverware sets" and camping gear. Try also different ways of sitting.

UNIT REVIEW

REVIEWING CONCEPTS:

Unity and diversity

1. Muslims everywhere share the same beliefs and Islamic customs.

2. Muslims live all over the world in different circumstances and have different ways of doing things.

Climate and geography

Contrast mountain and lowland, island, peninsula, coast, river and ocean, rainy, dry, city and village

People and languages

Different appearances of people; different ways of talking. Show pictures from library books of Muslims from various parts of the world.

Customs

Many different ways to have fun: review the customs described in the ten places. Have the students talk about, draw or show-and-tell customs in their country or family, recalling the Section 5 pre-reading activity for including all students' countries represented in the class (See page 60, #4).

Teach songs from Saida Chaudry's songbook *We Are Muslim Children* (American Trust Publications, 1984), especially "Little Friends in Other Lands," "Allah Loves the Children," "Baking Cookies for 'id," and "Call of Islam," or have students learn 'id songs known to the families of their classmates from various countries.

REVIEWING SKILLS:

Geography and Map Skills: Identifying the countries mentioned on a map

Use the map poster (map of the world, showing land and water masses with outlines and labels of the countries mentioned in section on one-color background) with Worksheets # 10, # 11 and # 12 to use in identification and matching game; The first worksheet contains each country outline in a size exactly matching that of the poster map, labeled within the outline with the country name. The second worksheet contains pictographs of the custom mentioned in the text. The third worksheet contains the names of the countries. The map is posted in the classroom, and the students cut out and color the countries and the pictographs, which are then matched to the places on the poster and attached with thumbtacks or removable tape. In the three-part game, students first match the shapes, then names, then customs.

Name _____   W O R K S H E E T   # 7

The Hajj

Match the words with what the pilgrims are doing in each picture.

| 4. | 1. | 5. |

| 3. |

| 2. |

1. Wearing *ihram*, pilgrim's clothes
2. Standing at Arafat
3. Throwing stones at Shaitan
4. Going around the Kaaba 7 times
5. Going from hill to hill like Hajar

Name _____   W O R K S H E E T   # 9 B

Questions for Gambian Village Map

Answer the questions and color the map on Worksheet #9A.

1. Trace the fence of the largest family compound in red.
   Whose family lives there? The chief's family

2. How many family compounds are in the village? (4)
   Trace the fence or each compound in blue.

3. How many houses are in the village? (17)

4. How many houses are round? (10) Color them yellow.

5. How many houses are not round? (7) Color them grey.

6. Where is the big tree? In the center of the village

7. Why is the tree important? People meet under it
   Color it green.

8. What building is north of the tree? Majid

9. Which road goes west from the village? To next village
   Color it red.

10. Which road goes east from the village? To fields
    Color it orange.

11. The fields are _____East_____ of the village.

12. The market place is _____South_____ of the village.
    Color it purple.

13. What important resource is east of the tree? The well
    Color it blue.

STORIES FOR ENRICHMENT

- Allah is Greatest
- The Idols
- Ibrahim's Father
- Hajar and Her Baby
- Ibrahim's Son
- Building the Kaaba

Part IV:

Student Activities

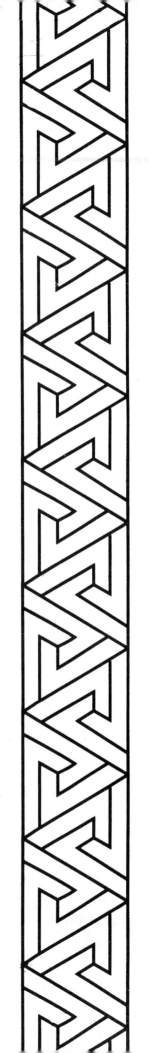

Allah is Greatest

The Qur'an tells the story of Ibrahim. Ibrahim was a very special young man. He worshiped Allah. His people worshiped idols. Ibrahim wanted to show his people that Allah is the Greatest. Allah showed him signs.

Ibrahim and his people looked up at the sky one night. They saw a beautiful star shining. Ibrahim said, "Could this be the Greatest? Could this be Allah?" But then, the star went out of sight. That couldn't be the Greatest!

Then they saw the moon come up in the sky. A bright, shining circle in the sky! "Could this be my Lord?" But then the moon set into the shadows, just like the star. He prayed that Allah would help them understand.

Then they saw the sun rise. The brightest light, like a fire lighting up the whole world! "Could this be my Lord? Could this be the Greatest?" But then, at the end of the day, the sun set. The light of the sun was gone. Darkness came again and his people saw the stars and the moon. They saw how they lit up the dark night. They saw the sun, the biggest thing in the sky. Sunshine made it warm and made everything grow.

But the stars, moon and sun went away. There must be something greater. Ibrahim knew that Allah, his Lord, made the stars, moon and sun. He made the land and the water. He made the trees and our food. He made all the animals and people. He made Ibrahim and his family. Allah made everything! Allah is the Greatest!

From Qur'an, 6:76-80

The Idols

Ibrahim's family and their friends didn't believe in Allah. They didn't know what Allah helped Ibrahim to understand. They used to pray to idols. They had some that were shaped like animals. They had some shaped like people. Some looked like monsters.

They believed that these idols helped them. They thought the idols could make it rain or make the sun shine. If they were sick, they asked the idols to make them well. Sometimes they put food and drinks in front of them.

Ibrahim told the people to believe in Allah. He told them Allah is the greatest. He told them that Allah created everything. He told them to stop praying to idols. He told the people they were wrong.

Those people got very angry at Ibrahim. He was a young man telling them what to do. He said, "I believe Allah is the greatest. You will see that you are wrong."

When the people went away, Ibrahim went to the idols and broke them. He did not break the biggest one. The people called that one the chief idol.

The people saw their idols broken. They were angry and scared. They brought Ibrahim and asked him, "Who did this to our gods?"

Ibrahim was very clever. He said, "The chief idol did it. Ask the idols, if they can talk."

They answered, "You know they cannot talk!"

So Ibrahim asked, "Why do you pray to something that can't talk or even help itself?" "You pray to these instead of Allah. But they can't help you or hurt you."

But the people didn't like to hear that they were wrong. They tried to burn Ibrahim. But Allah saved him from their fire.

From Qur'an, 21:51-71

Ibrahim's Father

Ibrahim's father was named Azar. Ibrahim loved him and wanted to help him. He was an idol-maker. He also believed that the idols could help people or hurt them. Azar worshipped the idols.

Ibrahim asked his father, "Why do you worship idols? They can't see, they can't make themselves. They can't help you or hurt you."

His father was angry. Ibrahim said, "Believe in Allah. I know something that you don't know. Allah helped me to understand. Don't follow the Satan! I don't want Allah to punish you."

Ibrahim's father was so angry that he forgot himself. He told Ibrahim, "You don't believe in my gods?" He said, "I will stone you if you don't stop talking about Allah!" Ibrahim's

father told him, "Go away from me for a long time!"

Was Ibrahim angry at his father? Did he try to hit him or say angry words back? No, Ibrahim was very sad. He wanted his father to believe in Allah. He wanted him to go to Paradise. Ibrahim asked Allah to forgive his father. He remembered his father's love and kindness when he was not angry.

From Qur'an, 6:75-80; 9:114; 19:41-48; 21:51-56; 26:77-86; 37:83- 99

Hajar and Her Baby

Prophet Ibrahim had a wife named Sarah. They lived together for many years. They still had no children. Sarah loved her husband, and she wanted him to be happy. She told him he could marry Hajar, her servant girl. Prophet Ibrahim married her. Hajar had a son named Ismael. When Sarah saw the baby, she felt jealous. She told Ibrahim to take Hajar and her son away.

Ibrahim took Hajar and her baby to a place in the desert called Makkah. Allah told Ibrahim to leave his wife Hajar and the baby. He left them alone in a dry valley between the mountains. He left them with some water. He believed that Allah would care for them.

After a while, the waterskin was empty. Hajar and her

baby Ismael were very thirsty. The baby cried. Hajar was afraid he would die. She went up one of the hills to look for signs of people. Perhaps some people would pass by and share their water. She came down and went up another hill to look. When she came back to Ismael, she found him almost dead. She went back and forth between the hills seven times. She was going back to her baby when she heard a voice. "Help us if you can," she said. It was the Angel Jibril's voice, sent by Allah! Jibril hit the earth with his heel. Water gushed out of the ground! Hajar was surprised. She began to dig in the ground. They drank and thanked Allah, who answered Hajar's prayer.

Hajar and Ismael stayed near the water. After a while, some people saw birds flying above the water. They came to Hajar and asked to stay with her. She told them the story. They put up their tents. They took care of Hajar and the baby.

The water that came to Hajar and Ismael is the well of Zamzam. After a long time, the well became covered up. Allah showed it to Prophet Muhammad's grandfather in a dream. He dug it up again. Since then, it has flowed. Pilgrims to Makkah still drink it today. Pilgrims walk where Hajar ran looking for water.

From Hadith Sahih Al Bukhari, 4:584

Ibrahim's Son

Ibrahim's son Ismael was very gentle and kind. Ibrahim loved him very much, as fathers love their children.

One night, Ibrahim had a dream. Ibrahim was a Prophet of Allah. Allah talks to Prophets in their dreams. So if Ibrahim saw something in a dream, he had to do that.

Ibrahim's dream told him to kill his son for Allah. The dream told him to sacrifice Ismael. Ibrahim knew he had to do it. He decided to talk to his son. One day, Ibrahim and Ismael were walking together. Ibrahim told his son, "My dear son, I had a dream. I saw in the dream that I have to sacrifice you." He asked his son, "What do you think about that?"

Ismael loved his father very much. He also loved Allah. He knew that his father had to obey Allah. He had to do what Allah told him. So he was very brave. He told his father, "Oh, my father, do what Allah commands. I will bear it, if Allah wills."

Ibrahim got ready with the knife. Ismael put his face down. They believed in Allah very much. But it was very, very hard for them.

Then something happened. A voice called Ibrahim! The voice said, "Oh Ibrahim! You have already obeyed me! You have done what the dream told."

Then, as Ibrahim and Ismael watched in surprise, a huge ram, like a big sheep with horns appeared. It was suddenly in the place where Ismael lay down to be killed!

Father and son were very happy. They killed the ram instead of Ismael, and they had a lot of good meat.

Allah didn't want Ismael to die. He wanted to test them. He wanted to see if they would obey. Father and son obeyed Allah together. He gave them a good reward.

From Qur'an, 37:99-109

Building the Kaaba

Prophet Ibrahim came to his son at Makkah, called Bakkah in those days. He and Ismael were thankful for Allah's mercy to their family. They built a house where people could worship Allah. They built it where Allah showed them.

Ibrahim and Ismael gathered stones from the mountains nearby. They dug in the earth to make the house stand firm. They cut and piled the stones. They put a special stone to mark one corner of the house.

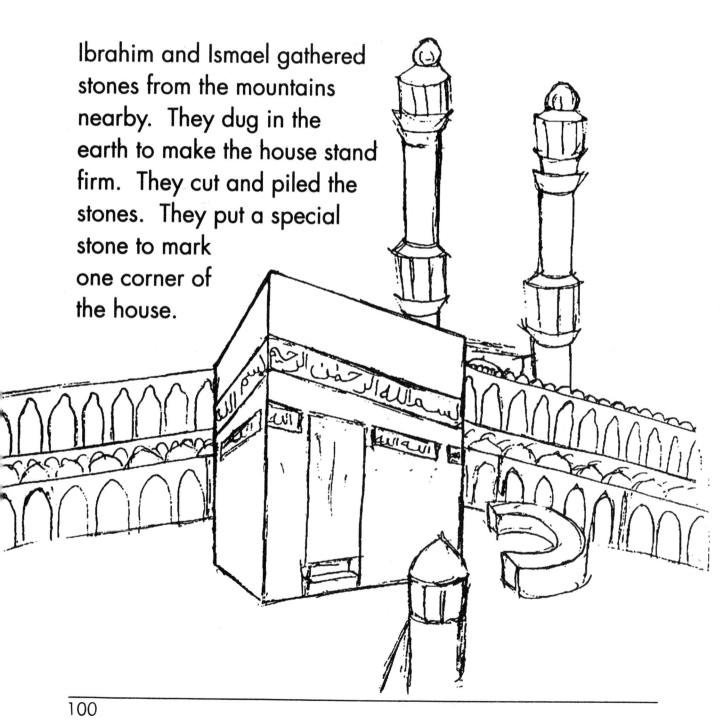

They built the four walls row by row. The walls rose higher. Ismael brought a rock for his father to stand on. Prophet Ibrahim stood on the rock to build the top of the walls.

Ibrahim prayed to Allah while they built the Kaaba. He said, "Accept the work from us." He asked Allah to make them and their families Muslims and show them how to worship. He asked Allah to make them and their people into a nation who loves and obeys Allah. He asked Allah to send a prophet from Ismael's sons and grandchildren and teach the people . He said "Make this place safe and give its believing people fruits and riches!"

You can make pilgrimage, or Hajj. You can visit the Kaaba that Ibrahim and Ismael built. You can go around the house seven times as they did. You can stand to pray where Prophet Ibrahim and his son stood.

From Qur'an 2:125-127; 3:96-97; 14:37-41; Hadith Sahih Al Bukhari, 4:584

Trace the outline and color in the words of this Islamic *eid* greeting.

Blessed celebration!
Eid mubarak!

Trace and say the names of the two Islamic celebrations:

1. Eid al-Fitr

2. Eid al-Adha

عيد الفطر

عيد الأضحى

Eid greeting

Use this page for greeting cards or to trace and decorate.

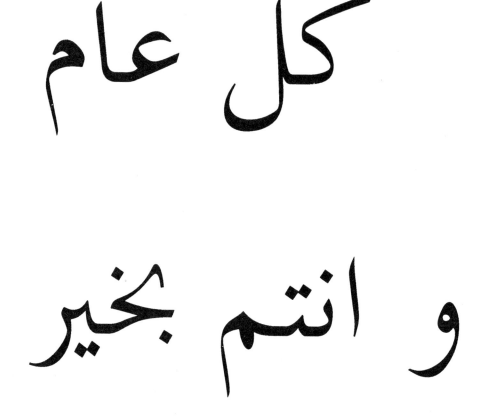

Kul amm wa antum bi khair!
May every year find you in good health!

Eid greeting

Eid greeting in Arabic to trace, color

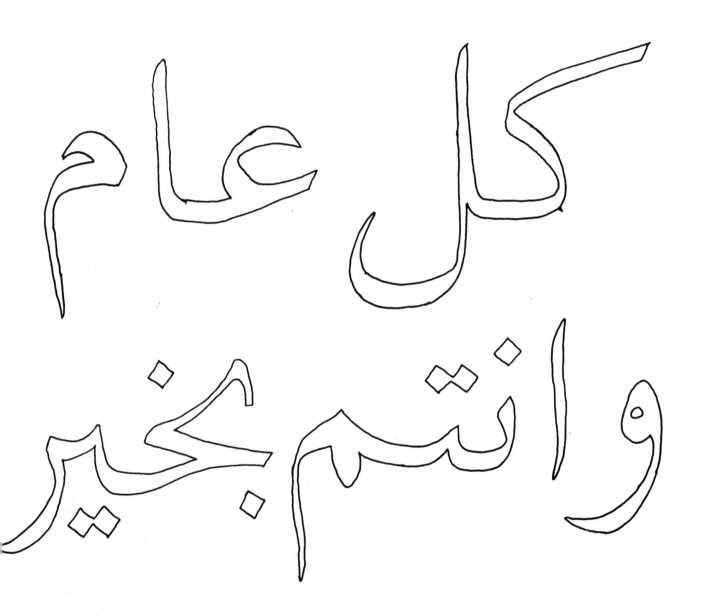

Kul amm wa antum bi khair!
May every year find you in good health!

The Moon's Changes Each Month

1. Cut out the moon strip the full length of the paper. Add another strip of the same width and length. Mount on cardboard strip of the same size.

2. Seal a business envelope and slit open both ends.

3. In the middle of one side, carefully cut a window the same size as one section of the moon diagram.

4. Slide the moon strip into the envelope so that the first segment of the moon's phases shows in the window.

5. Slide the diagram slowly past the window to show the class the moon's phases in "animination."

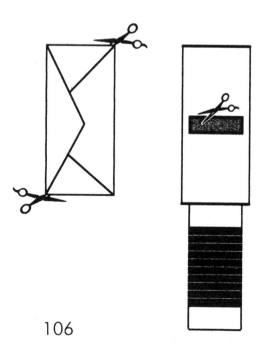

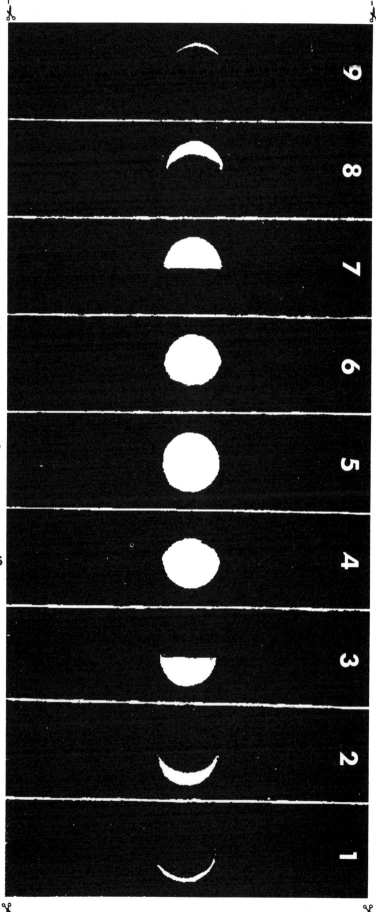

Months of the Islamic Calendar Year

Practice writing the names of the months on the line in front of each number

_____ 1.   محرم   Muharram

_____ 2.   صفر   Safar

_____ 3.   ربيع الأول   Rabi 1

_____ 4.   ربيع الأخر   Rabi 2

_____ 5.   جمادى الأولى   Jumad 1

_____ 6.   جمادى الأخرة   Jumad 2

_____ 7.   رجب   Rajab

_____ 8.   شعبان   Sha'ban

_____ 9.   رمضان   Ramadan

_____ 10.   شوال   Shawwal

_____ 11.   ذو القعدة   Zulqaidah

_____ 12.   ذو الحجة   Zulhijjah

The Hajj

Match the words with what the pilgrims are doing in each picture.

1. Wearing *ihram,* pilgrim's clothes
2. Standing at Arafat
3. Throwing stones at Shaitan
4. Going around the Kaaba 7 times
5. Going from hill to hill like Hajar

Cut the story into sentence strips as follows:

✂ -

A poor woman made bread for the Prophet.

✂ -

She had only a little flour.

She had only a little oil.

✂ -

The Prophet tasted the woman's bread.

The bread tasted very good.

✂ -

It tasted good because the poor woman loved the Prophet.

Prophet Muhammad thanked and blessed her.

✂ -

An African Village in the Gambia

masjid

chief's compound

← to next village

meeting tree

to fields →

well

to river →

to city

toilet

wash room

N

W — E

S

market place

Questions for Gambian Village Map

Answer the questions and color the map on Worksheet #9A.

1. Trace the fence of the largest family compound in red. Whose family lives there?

2. How many family compounds are in the village? Trace the fence or each compound in blue.

3. How many houses are in the village?

4. How many houses are round?_____ Color them yellow.

5. How many houses are not round?____Color them grey.

6. Where is the big tree?

7. Why is the tree important? Color it green.

8. What building is north of the tree?

9. Which road goes west from the village? Color it red.

10. Which road goes east from the village? Color it orange.

11. The fields are _____ of the village.

12. The market place is _____ of the village. Color it purple.

13. What important resource is east of the tree? Color it blue.

Country Outlines

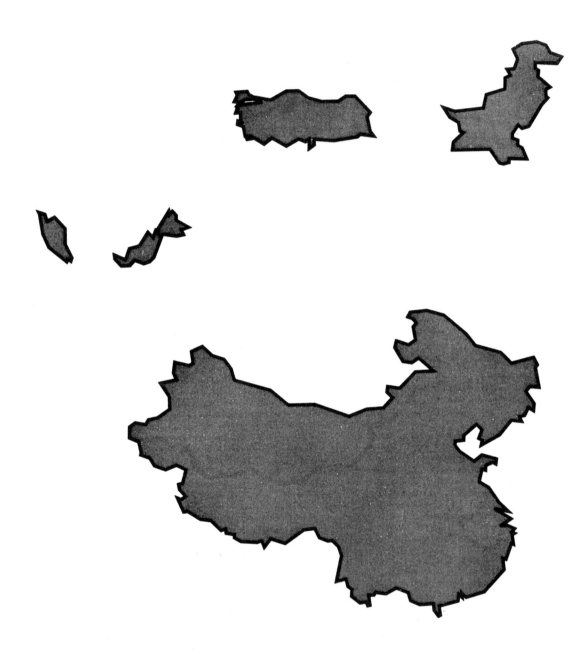

Country Outlines

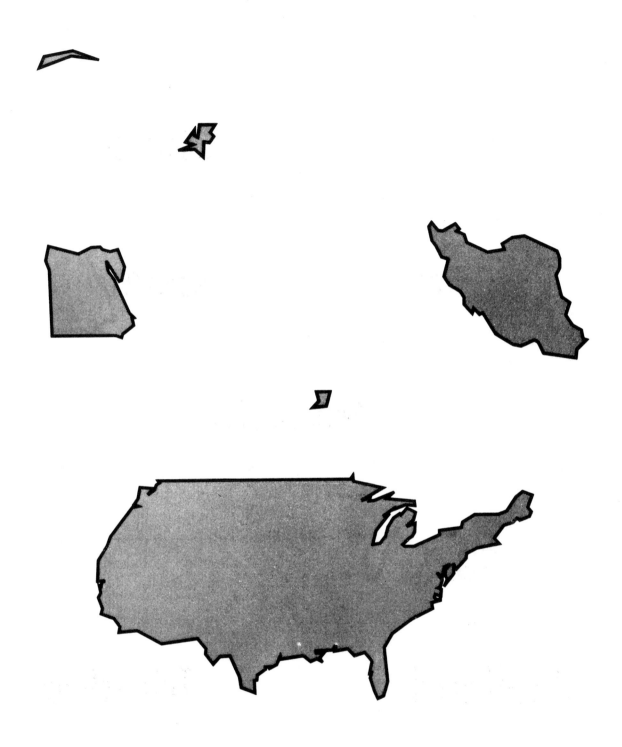

Country Names

Cut out and place on poster map to identify countries.

Iran   China

Pakistan   Gambia

Malaysia

Egypt   Turkey

Holland   Trinidad

United States

Custom Pictographs

Cut out and place on poster map.

NOTES